D1145066

LANCASHIRE COUNTY LIBRARY
SOUTH EAST LANCS.

WORLD WAR I COLLECTION

This book should be returned to any branch of the
Lancashire County Library on or before the date shown

ACCRINGTON
- 7 DEC 2006

1 9 DEC 2006
- 6 MAR 2007
- 8 MAY 2007

1 4 JUL 2008
- 5 JUN 2009

Lancashire County Library
Bowran Street
Preston PR1 2UX

Lancashire
County Council

www.lancashire.gov.uk/libraries

Lancashire County Library
30118103800813

LL1(A)

UNCLE CHARLIE COMES HOME

UNCLE CHARLIE COMES HOME

Westerham and the Great War,
1914–1918

David Bateman

Book Guild Publishing
Sussex, England

103800813   10|06

LANCASHIRE COUNTY LIBRARY
SOUTH EAST LANCS.

First published in Great Britain in 2006 by
The Book Guild Ltd
25 High Street
Lewes, East Sussex
BN7 2LU

Copyright © David Bateman 2006

The right of David Bateman to be identified as the author of
this work has been asserted by him in accordance with the
Copyright, Designs and Patents Act 1988.

All rights reserved. No part of this publication may be reproduced, transmitted, or stored
in a retrieval system, in any form or by any means, without permission in writing from
the publisher, nor be otherwise circulated in any form of binding or cover other than that
in which it is published and without a similar condition being imposed on the subsequent
purchaser.

Typesetting in Times by
Acorn Bookwork Ltd, Salisbury, Wiltshire

Printed in Great Britain by
CPI Bath

A catalogue record for this book is available from
The British Library.

ISBN 1 84624 019 0

*This book is dedicated to
a brave generation from
Westerham who went to war,
remembering especially the fifty
who did not come home*

Contents

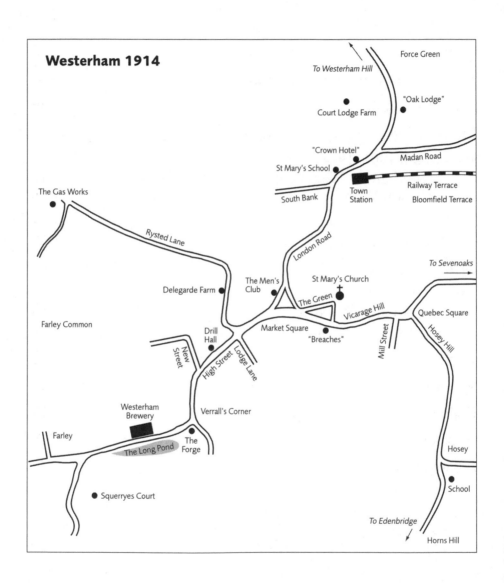

The Western Front

England

• Dover

Dunkirk •

Belgium

Calais •

Ypres
•

Boulogne •

Messines
•

France

Loos •

Arras •

Cambrai •

Abbeville •

River Somme

Albert
•

St Quentin

Dieppe •

Amiens
•

— — — Front Line 1916

THE WAR.

A

Public Meeting

Will be held in the

DRILL HALL, WESTERHAM,

At 8.15 p.m.,

On Monday, September 7th,

With the object of explaining the reasons

WHY ENGLAND HAS GONE TO WAR,

And why it is of vital importance in the present grave
National emergency that

EVERY ABLE-BODIED MAN OF SUITABLE AGE

should respond to Lord Kitchener's call for a further

ARMY OF 100,000 MEN.

All, men and women alike, are cordially invited to attend.

THE CHAIR AT THE MEETING WILL BE TAKEN BY

LORD WEARDALE.

SPEAKERS:

H. W. FORSTER, Esq., M.P.,

A. W. SMITHERS, Esq., J.P.,

A. E. d'AVIGDOR GOLDSMID, Esq., J.P., C.C.,

E. C. GOLDBERG, Esq.

GOD SAVE THE KING.

Poster 1914

X

Foreword and Acknowledgements

I often look at war memorials. To stand on a village green or in a country churchyard anywhere in England and view the seriate names of those who died between 1914 and 1918 invariably provokes a sense of awe and disbelief. How could so many men be lost to such small communities in the space of just four years? What pain and suffering was endured by the inhabitants? All too often the sadness is compounded by repeated surnames indicating brothers or at least members of the same family who did not come home. What could it have been like to have lived through those times? What courage and resolution was required from the generation who raised a citizen army, which then fought and won a Continental war?

The town of Westerham in Kent is typical of many who sent their young men to that war and then suffered the consequential loss. Growing up in my home town of Westerham in the 1950s, I could scarcely be unaware that the local war memorial listed a C.A. Bateman, the fourth name among 50. What began as an enquiry into my uncle's history grew quite naturally to encompass all those names that are listed on the memorial and, gradually, this evolved into a story of how a small community went to war; of the bravery of those who marched away and the courage of those who remained at home. Although the town of Westerham is the theme of this volume, the story could be that of any town or village in England and though 'Uncle Charlie' is its inspiration, it is also the story of every man who fought in the Great War.

It is appropriate at this point to acknowledge the help and enthusiasm of many Westerham people in producing this book. Thanks must go to David Matthews of Westways for discovering and reproducing many of the excellent photographs that appear in the volume and for his encouragement in bringing it to publication. Thanks also to Geraint Jenkins for painstakingly reading the earlier drafts and for correcting my grammatical howlers, admittedly acquired at Westerham School. Alan Taylor Smith of the Westerham Society has also been very supportive and helpful on many occasions, especially by allowing access to the 'Streatfeild Papers'. Thank you to Joy Lee for unravelling the complexities of the Haggard and Currie families of 'Breaches', Vicarage Hill, and thanks also to Fred Wood of Ash Road for sorting out the many Wood families of French Street and elsewhere. Lastly, a big thank you to Peter Finch of Quebec Square, a source of so much local knowledge, who has given constant help and encouragement throughout.

David Bateman
Rownhams, Southampton

Author's Note

The identities of Westerham soldiers named within the narrative and the Roll of Honour have been gathered from a number of sources. At the beginning of each of the war years, the *Westerham Herald* produced a nominal roll of all those serving in uniform and this has formed the basis of all who are mentioned. Despite the majority of First World War service records no longer existing, the medal entitlements of those who served overseas between 1914 and 1918 are held at the National Archives and, wherever possible, names have been checked against these lists. The Medal Index Cards are a complete alphabetical record of the millions who served in the Great War and besides name, rank and number often give the date of proceeding overseas, battalions and regiments in which served, ranks achieved and whether discharged through wounds or sickness. Sadly, where a John Smith or a William Jones occurs, there are often too many of the same name for a positive identity.

The addresses of those who served are also problematical. There are frequent and typical references in wartime *Westerham Heralds* to 'Arthur F—, whose parents live in the High Street, being home from the Front' or that 'George H— of London Road is reported wounded'. Men of military age were often working away from home by the time of their enlistment so that place of residence may not always be strictly correct. Some street locations given may also refer to immediately pre war or post war addresses. There are also a surprising number of families relocating within Westerham even during the war years. In most cases house numbers have also been avoided as many streets have been renumbered on more than one occasion. Mill Street, off Quebec Square, was originally Mill Lane and here the later name is used.

Hopefully readers will forgive any errors and omissions.

Surviving service records and unit war diaries held at National

Archives have been invaluable in many instances and these include:

Arthur Horace Lang WO 339 23930 and WO 95 1263
John Alfred Pigou Inglis WO 95 1925
Ian Campbell Penney WO 95 1946
Arthur Baldry WO 95 2805
Ernest Wood WO 95 3025
Percy Beresford WO 95 3001
George Alfred Hider WO 364
George Harry Fennell WO 363

Many of the Westerham photographs belong to the 'Evenden' collection and are reproduced by permission of Westerham Parish Council. The photographs of AG Douglas and JA Pigou Inglis are reproduced courtesy of Rugby School and that of AH Lang courtesy of Harrow School. Many of the soldier portraits have been kindly lent by the families.

The extract from Churchill's speech of April 1925 on p.xix is reproduced with permission of Curtis Brown Ltd, London on behalf of The Estate of Winston Churchill. © Winston S. Churchill.

Every effort has been made to gain permission for information used within this book. The author apologises for any omissions and will endeavour to acknowledge these at the earliest opportunity.

Introduction

From a very early age I was aware that my father kept in his possession an envelope containing some medals, an army cap badge and a fading sepia photograph of a young soldier. Although seldom seen or referred to, these were the surviving memorabilia of my father's elder brother who as a young man was among the many thousands who marched away to the Great War of 1914–1918 and did not return. When in later years I began to question my father on what had befallen his brother, his answers invariably began, 'We could never find out. We were never told. We never knew...' This apparent mystery, which had always haunted my father's family, was to be the starting point of a trail of enquiry that would lead to years of studying numerous accounts of the First World War, of days of poring over surviving documents and of walking the bleak windswept fields of northern France. As parts of the mystery unfolded this, in turn, would lead to perhaps a beginning of comprehension of a war that engulfed the whole of Europe, of a holocaust that would see three quarters of a million British dead and in particular the sacrifice of one small English market town.

Few communities are without a memorial to the dead of the two world wars, from major towns with vast panelled edifices to small villages where a plaque or tablet within the parish church suffices to carry the names of those from the locality who made the supreme sacrifice. The war memorial at Westerham stands within the churchyard just beyond the church porch. Erected by public subscription in 1920, the memorial consists of a crucifix surmounting an octagonal plinth, which looks out over the Darent valley. Recorded on the sides of the plinth are the names of 50 men of the parish who died in the Great War. The memorial was extended after 1945 to include those who died in the Second World War. In common with most memorials, the numbers listed for the First World War are twice that of the

Second. Every November at Westerham's Remembrance Sunday service the names inscribed on the memorial are read out to the congregation: 'George Walter Allen, Arthur Baldry, George William Barnett...', the sad litany continues to 'Ernest Wood and George Obed Wood'. That total of 50 men came from a Westerham population which in 1914 numbered little more than 3,000. From the men of military age the proportion is even more devastating. Nearly one in five of those who marched away did not come home. From a distance of nearly 90 years it is difficult to gauge the degree of heartbreak caused to a small community like Westerham but great it surely must have been. Those listed range in age from 18-year-old George Walter Allen from Mill Street to 46-year-old Ambrose Langley Hunt from Westerham Hill. Nineteen of the Westerham fallen were married men, a further ten were aged 21 years or under; remarkably, two were ordained priests. The nature of First World War fighting meant that many of the dead were never found. Their bodies were simply lost to the battlefield, swallowed up in the Flanders mud or atomised in a storm of iron shards and explosives. Among those never properly accounted for are 16 men named on the memorial. That number includes my father's elder brother, Charles Albert Bateman, who enlisted as a young 'Territorial' in 1914 and was later posted missing, presumed killed, aged 20 in 1918. There are family names on the memorial that have existed in Westerham for centuries and names that endure to this day.

Yet Westerham's commitment to the war was not just in those who died. There is evidence of more than 350 men from the town serving in uniform between 1914 and 1918 from whom at least 50 were wounded to a severity that required repatriation to England. The identification of these Westerham men is far from straightforward. Human memory is failing with the passage of years and the majority of papers pertaining to First World War servicemen no longer exist. In November 1940, an incendiary bomb that hit the Army Records Centre in London destroyed nearly all the service records of those who served in the Great War. Those documents that survived have been painstakingly restored in recent years but still only account for around a quarter of the total and are often incomplete and difficult to read. Even a search among local records is not helped by the proliferation of surnames like Wood (around ten families in Westerham in 1914) and the penchant for changing first names – Johns becoming Jacks, Henrys becoming Harrys and vice-versa. Yet out of piecemeal evidence, an extraordinary story has emerged of local pride and stoicism together with a wealth of individual heroism, courage and endurance.

Despite having passed into history, the First World War is still surprisingly close. The often-seen flickering newsreel footage may appear to come from another age, yet there are still a handful of men alive (no more than a dozen in 2005) who actually took part. Many older Westerham citizens will have memories of relatives who fought in the Great War and particularly of those who later became leading members of the community. Many in Westerham are sons and daughters of the First War generation. As a schoolboy in Westerham in the 1950s, I can recall talking to a number of local men who served in the Great War. I hope I listened to their reminiscences with politeness even if without great attention. I wish I could speak to them now – there is so much I would want to ask them. There was Bernard Johnson of Westbury Terrace, Mr Wylde, a teacher at Westerham School, Mr Turnage of Trotts Lane – a regular soldier in 1914 who recalled the euphoria of being brought home from India only to wish they had stayed where they were – Laurence Crisp of London Road, who served in France with the Royal Engineers and never came home once in three years, and Bill Holland, latterly Westerham's gravedigger, who used to extol the 'delights' of the Armenian girls he encountered while serving in the Middle East. The lasting impression of these veterans was of sparky upright characters who were proud of their achievements and of having been part of an earth-changing event. They spoke of pride in their regiments (of the West Kent's innate superiority over the Buffs) and of endurance in adversity that set them apart from other men. None of these men considered themselves victims, just grateful that they had been spared to return home to pick up the threads of their lives when many of their comrades had not.

Yet today it often seems that this war, if thought about at all, has become synonymous with mud, carnage, incompetence, futility and waste. Callous generals, lambs led to slaughter, lions led by donkeys; all sum up many of the prevailing mantras on the First World War. The war was undoubtedly a ghastly business; Britain's casualties exceeded anything in our history, either before or mercifully since. Yet while the war was certainly a tragedy, the degree to which it could have been avoided must remain debatable. The countdown to conflict after the Sarajevo assassinations might have been halted had any goodwill been shown on all sides. Sadly it was not. Troops were already on the march before Britain declared war. That Britain could have stood by while France was defeated was as unlikely in 1914 as it was in 1940. A German fleet based on the Atlantic coast of France, threatening Britain's sea lanes, would be no more acceptable in the First World War than it was in the Second, and if it was right to go to war for Poland in 1939 then it is arguably right that Britain should go to war when Belgium was similarly invaded in August 1914. Hindsight is a luxury available only to future historians.

The true tragedy for Britain is surely that never before in our history has this country raised an army of Continental proportions and then taken the consequential casualties. As a primarily naval power, Britain had always made do with a small army raised from volunteers and mainly utilised to police the Empire. In the space of four years from 1914, the army expanded from around 200,000 men to one of over 4 million. That army also went to war at a time when the weapons that could be brought to bear on static troops (e.g. the bomb, mine, artillery and later poisoned gas) had reached a peak of efficiency whereas the only weapon of mobility was the same as a thousand years before – the horse. It is not therefore so surprising that our soldiers then took such horrendous casualties. What is more remarkable is the courage, the stoicism and the sense of duty with which our mainly citizen army stuck to its task in achieving a stunning victory in 1918. Nor should the resolve and support of the community they left behind be forgotten.

It is hard therefore to dismiss the sacrifice of so many men, including the 50 men of Westerham in terms of mere blunder and stupidity. The loss of three quarters of a million men from this country cannot be dismissed lightly but it should always be remembered that France suffered twice as many casualties and a large part of its territory was occupied. Germany's losses were greater again and it also suffered the defeat and humiliation that led to Hitler and National Socialism. Britain did not suffer the defeat and starvation of the Austrians, nor did it suffer the fate of Russia, where the war led to a revolution that enslaved her people for the next 80 years. The right to continue our own way of life, unaltered, is the great legacy of the men who fought in the Great War, a legacy guaranteed by another generation just 20 years later, and for which we have much to be grateful. A man who would later become a famous citizen of Westerham, a Mr Winston Churchill, would of course better articulate these sentiments. On 25 April 1925, at the unveiling of the memorial to the Royal Naval Division at Horse Guards Parade, his address included these words:

> We are often tempted to ask ourselves what we have gained by the enormous sacrifice made by those to whom this memorial is erected. But this was never the issue with those who marched away. No question of advantage presented itself to their minds ... They only saw the light shining clear on the path of duty. They never asked the question 'What shall we gain?' They only asked the question 'Where lies the right?' It was thus that they marched away for ever.

These words equally apply to our own memorial and the 50 men of Westerham. They and the many more who served and were lucky enough to return are part of our history and our heritage. They deserve to be remembered with admiration, with pride and with gratitude.

Westerham 1901–1914

At the accession of Edward VII, following the death of Queen Victoria in 1901, Westerham was part of a nation that had seen no major war or threat to national security for almost a century. Since Waterloo in 1815, such wars that had taken place could often be classed as little more than colonial skirmishes. Clashes in the Sudan with rebel tribesmen or unrest on the North-West Frontier were few and far between and were often over before events could be properly reported at home. Even the comparatively major conflicts like the Crimean War and the Boer War (still to run its course in 1901) took place on distant shores and while the casualties were cause for concern, the outcome was never in serious doubt. In all these sundry wars of the nineteenth century, more men died from disease and sickness than from Russian shells or Boer Mausers. Safe behind the world's largest navy and backed by industrial might based on seaborne trade, Britain and her distant armies always won through in the end. Involvement in European conflicts like the Franco-Prussian War of 1870–1871 had been successfully avoided. When Westerham celebrated King Edward VII's coronation on 9 August 1902, its citizens saw no reason why another 100 years of peace and security could not ensue. That special day was marked by celebrations that included a peal of bells and a special service at the parish church, which was followed by a dinner held on The Green for all the Westerham citizens over 50 years of age. Nearly 240 attended to be waited on by younger members of the community. Any visitor to the town that day observing the festivities would note a small Kentish market town of moderate prosperity set in a secure and well ordered society.

A national census taken in 1901 shows the parish of Westerham as a sub-district of Sevenoaks and having a population on 31 March of 2,360. A largely rural community at the western edge of Kent and 20 miles south of London,

Westerham was established around a church and village green at the junction of roads leading to Sevenoaks, Oxted, Edenbridge and Bromley. The majority of houses were strung out along the east-west roads leading from the market square with small concentrations of dwellings at Quebec Square, New Street, Lodge Lane and Duncan's Yard. Newer housing developments had more recently been established at Madan Road off the main route leading north to London. The census, which also includes the citizens' occupations, lists carters, blacksmiths, bricklayers, shop workers, publicans and draymen. But above all, the overriding industry of the district was agriculture with cowmen, nurserymen, farm workers and gardeners exceeding all other trades. Farms ringed the town at Squerryes, Covers, Gayshams, Betsoms, Force Green, Charmans and Dunsdale. Nurseries stretched either side of the London Road supplying produce that was often dispatched to London via the local railway branch line, which had opened in 1881. A rough count of the census shows 70 men in trades from market gardener to nursery foreman while more than 80 had farm professions. Many of these workers were resident on the farms in the outlying districts. The big manor houses of Squerryes Court, Squerryes Lodge, Valence, Dunsdale and Court Lodge were major employers of domestic staff and even smaller houses such as Farley Croft and Marwell included cooks and parlour maids on their establishment. The census lists well over 100 residents of the town as working in domestic service. The brewery of Messrs Bushell, Watkins and Smith in the High Street was another significant industry with over 20 local employees. The census also lists a generation of 5 to 10-year-old schoolboys who, within a few short years, would have to face the awful test of a world war.

By far the longest enduring institution of the town was the thirteenth-century church of St Mary the Virgin where between 1900 and 1920 the Reverend Sydney Le Mesurier residing at the vicarage held the office of parish priest. He would officiate through the heartbreak of the war years that still lay some way ahead in 1901. For those of a non-conformist persuasion there was also a Congregational church, opened in1837, situated at the top of Fuller's Hill. There were two established state schools in the town: St Mary's for the girls in the London Road while the boys made the long walk to Hosey – on the road to Edenbridge and well remembered by generations of Westerham youngsters. In 1901 Edith Davis was resident in the School House at St Mary's while at Hosey the headmaster was George Barrett, a post later held in the war years by Mr Forsey.

By today's standards the workers' lives in the Edwardian era were hard and unremitting, usually for low wages and often against a background of overcrowded housing. Many cottages in New Street and Mill Street list an astonishing eight and ten occupants, in some cases spread across three generations. 'Lodging' was quite commonplace for any who had a spare room and, almost as a rule, those who resided in Westerham also worked there.

For the ordinary working people of the town there were a number of diversions from the daily grind. There were thriving football and cricket clubs, the secretary of the latter being a Mr Horton, who owned the timber business adjacent to the station yard. At least two horticultural societies existed, one of which was under the stewardship of Walter Rowe, the head gardener at Squerryes Court. The town also supported eight public houses of which the Crown, opposite the station, the Warde Arms and The Rifleman in the High Street have long since disappeared. In 1914 a motion picture cinema was opened just off Quebec Square offering novel entertainment with seats from as little as 3d (1p). There was also a Working Men's Club, which is still in existence today.

Another enduring institution to which many Westerham men belonged was the local detachment of the 1st Volunteer Battalion of the Royal West Kent Regiment. As far back as 1883 there are records of a company of Rifle Volunteers based in Westerham with a headquarters at the Town Hall in the High Street. Local men aged 17 to 45 could enlist in the Volunteers for part-time soldiering with weekly drill, occasional weekend exercises and the added bonus of an annual summer camp. The reward was a small remuneration, camaraderie and healthy outdoor activity. In 1900,

3

H Company of the 1st V.B. Royal West Kents numbered 70 'effectives' drawn from the Westerham area. Company orders were posted in Westerham's local paper, the *Herald*, at the beginning of each month. Parade and training took place at Company HQ on Thursday evenings and new recruits were trained on Tuesdays. Musketry training took place one Saturday a month on the range at Westerham Hill. A professional instructor was attached to the Westerham Volunteers, invariably a drill sergeant of the parent regiment. In 1901, Sergeant James Leury of the Royal West Kents, a time-served soldier, held this post while living with his family in South Bank. Prior to the war years the resident instructor was Sergeant Thomas Henry Martle of Stratton Terrace. In time of war or national emergency, the Volunteers would be mobilised for garrison duty at home, thereby releasing the regulars for service overseas. However, as recently as the Boer War, volunteers from the Westerham Company had served in South Africa with the regulars of the 2nd Battalion, Royal West Kents. In 1908, the Volunteers were reorganised into the Territorial Army, becoming H Company of the 4th Battalion, Royal West Kent Regiment.

In 1904 a Cadet Corps was attached to the Westerham Volunteers, embodied by an Army Order, and known as the Westerham and Chipstead Cadet Corps, Royal West Kent Regiment. The unit was born out of a Church Lads Brigade founded a year earlier by Percy Beresford, the curate of St Mary's church. Aside from his church duties, Beresford, who lived on the London Road, was also a serving officer in the Territorial Army. The Cadet Corps was open to all schoolboys in the district. Besides the military aspects of the training, the unit sought to instil fitness and smartness amongst the boys as well as a sense of pride and identity with the Corps, the community and the country. Percy Beresford, a man of strong character and high ideals, as his subsequent war record would prove, strove to promote character and a sense of duty among the boys. His work with the Cadets would have a profound influence on a generation of Westerham youngsters in the years leading up to the First World War.

The Queen's Own Royal West Kent Regiment to which the Westerham Volunteers and Cadets belonged was a typical infantry unit of the pre-war British Army. The regiment came into being in 1881 when the old numbered regiments of foot were paired and in most cases given county affiliations, the 50th and 97th Regiments becoming the 1st and 2nd Battalions, Royal West Kent. At the time of this radical reorganisation, large and populated counties like Lancashire and Yorkshire were given up to six or seven new regiments while smaller counties had one or in some cases shared a regiment (e.g. The Notts and Derby Regiment). Surrey and Kent each had two regiments, largely on account of their proximity to the London recruiting area. These were The Queen's (Royal West Surrey) Regiment and the East Surreys, and The Buffs (East Kent Regiment) and The Royal West Kents. As its name implies, the Royal West Kents' recruiting area was that part of Kent west from the county town of Maidstone, where the barracks and headquarters were located, and extending into the London suburbs as far as New Cross and Lewisham. In peacetime the regiment consisted of two regular battalions, one of which would be stationed overseas garrisoning the Empire in any one of a dozen locations from Gibraltar to India and Hong Kong. The other 'homeservice' battalion was typically based at a military town like Aldershot or Shorncliffe and was often called upon to provide drafts to maintain the establishment of its foreign service counterpart. This meant that the homeservice battalion was often under strength but in time of war or national emergency the ranks would be made up by mobilising Reservists. Any man with recent military service invariably spent several years on the Reserve list. In peacetime this involved nothing more arduous than attendance at annual training but in time of national emergency these men were immediately recalled to duty. The Regiments 3rd Battalion was not an embodied unit but consisted of those men who remained at the barracks for training and recruiting and was also a holding unit for men on the Reserve. The 4th Battalion, to which Westerham's H Company belonged, was a Territorial Army unit consisting of part-time volunteers, having its headquarters at the

5

Corn Exchange, Tonbridge. There was also a 5th Territorial Battalion of part-timers centred on Bromley. Westerham's affiliation with the county regiment would have great significance in the war that lay ahead.

For the first decade of the twentieth century the life of Westerham continued the even tenor of its way. Local businesses plied their trade, farms and nurseries observed a routine dictated by the seasons, and civic organisations met and ordered their respective affairs. The daily needs of the community were met, almost exclusively, by the community itself. Heating and light was supplied by the Westerham Gas and Coke Company from their works on the Croydon Road, while Mr Horton supplied coal from his depot in the station yard. Mr Taylor's garage in the High Street serviced the transport requirements of the populace – cars and delivery vehicles for those who could afford them, bicycles for everyone else. Equestrian servicing was carried out by George Verrall at his forge at the corner of Mill Lane, his name being perpetuated at the bend in the High Street where his forge once stood. A complete range of individual shops around the market square catered for all life's essentials: Hollingsworth greengrocers, Hale's general stores, groceries at the 'International', meat from Mr Boddy's butcher shop, bread from Mills and Boreham's bakeries, clothing from Outrim's and household furnishings from Mr Shawyer's Stores. The diversity of local services ranged from Hookers the Printers and Mrs Parkhurst's kindergarten to Dr Russell's surgery and John Newman the chimney sweep. Each January, local organisations held a round of general meetings and annual dinners: the Gardeners' Club held their AGM at the King's Arms, as did the Bowling Club (President Mr A.B. Bell). The Westerham Tradesmen's Association held an annual dinner also at the King's Arms while the Men's Club met at the clubhouse. The Westerham Town Band (Albert Newton, bandmaster) advertised themselves as available for functions within a seven-mile radius of the town. The local schools followed their tried and trusted routines while the sportsmen changed from football to cricket at the end of every April.

Yet in 1911 there was something to celebrate. Not only would this be a coronation year, Edward VII having died the previous May, but also a local hero was about to be commemorated. This notable year began on 2 January with the unveiling of a statue on The Green to Westerham's hero of Quebec, General Wolfe. James Wolfe was born in Westerham in 1727 and went on to command the British forces in Canada during the Seven Years War. In 1759 he was to lead the British Army in the capture of Quebec, defeating the French but losing his life at the moment of victory. Now, 150 years later and thanks to public subscription, a striking bronze statue was erected on The Green to perpetuate his memory. (Up to recent years at least, no child could leave a Westerham school unversed in the story of Wolfe, Quebec and the storming of the Heights of Abraham.) The occasion was one for great civic pride. The Territorials of H Company paraded, as did the Cadets, the firemen and the Town Band. Guest of honour was the legendary 'old soldier', Lord Roberts of Kandahar who performed the unveiling before a large assembly of townspeople. The proceedings began with an address of welcome by Mr Shawyer, chairman of the Parish Council, and concluded with a public luncheon in the town hall at which Colonel Warde of Squerryes presided and Lord Roberts and Lord Strathcona were guests of honour.

The coronation of King George V on Thursday 22 June of the same year was occasioned by the death of Edward VII in May 1910. Then, in sombre mood, an assembly of citizens had gathered on The Green to hear Colonel Warde read the 'Proclamation' announcing the death of King Edward and the succession of George V. On the day of the state funeral, Friday 7 May 1910, Westerham paid its own respects to the late king. A procession which included the Cadets, the Territorials, the local firemen under Mr Hooker and led by the Town Band, made its way from the High Street to St Mary's church where a memorial service was held before a large congregation. The events of the day were solemnly reported in a black-edged *Westerham Herald*.

By contrast, Westerham's celebration of the coronation was part of a day of national rejoicing. The day's events commenced

7

with a peal of bells from the church followed by a combined coronation service led by the Reverend Le Mesurier and in which the Congregational church minister read the lesson. The service was followed by a gathering on The Green at which Colonel Warde addressed the townspeople, and the speeches concluded with the singing of the national anthem. The afternoon programme of sports and fancy dress was somewhat marred by persistent rain – a scenario that may well evoke memories of the 1953 coronation for some readers. The day concluded with a procession through a flag-bedecked town and the firing of a huge bonfire on Farley Common which was lit by Master John Warde.

The year of 1914 would begin much like any other. There were the usual round of general meetings and annual dinners held by the various clubs and civic bodies. The Choral Society held a concert at the town hall in which various instrumentalists and vocalists took part. The annual 'Wolfe' dinner was held at the George and Dragon Inn, at which Field Marshal Sir John French (later to command the British Expeditionary Force in France) was guest of honour. The guest list for the dinner, at which Colonel Warde presided, included prominent local citizens as well as officers from a number of regiments and representatives from Canada. The Town Band was also in attendance.

In March 1914, there was great excitement at the opening of a motion picture hall, The Swan Cinema, in premises near the bottom of Hosey Hill. The first performance on Wednesday 4 March was a drama called *When the Earth Trembled*, which played to a large audience. March of that year also saw heavy rain causing severe flooding in Quebec Square and Bloomfield Terrace.

By the summer of 1914 there was little evidence of the cataclysm that would soon engulf the world. Westerham was a community still very much at peace. Rumblings of unrest in the far off Balkans were occasionally reported but that was nothing new. The town's routine continued much as usual. On Whit Monday 1914, the Westerham cricketers played the Midland Railway Company at Squerryes, the home side losing by

88 runs. On 10 June the Cadet Corps held its annual inspection at Farley Common and on the 24th the Territorials took part in a torchlit procession at the neighbouring village of Brasted. This latter event was occasioned by the opening of the new Darent Valley Swimming Baths on land adjacent to the Brasted recreation ground. Amid great festivity, which was followed by gala swimming, the Baths were opened by Lord Stanhope of Chevening. In a slight departure from the planned programme, a campaigner for women's suffrage ran along the side of the pool shouting, 'Votes for women!'. When attempts were made to apprehend her, the protester retreated to the diving tower, hotly pursued by a member of the Tonbridge Swimming Club. After a brief struggle on the top board both protester and swimmer fell into the pool whereupon the protest became more of a rescue. With commendable British phlegm the proceedings continued unfazed. The ceremony ended with a procession in which the Westerham Band participated and at the conclusion of the celebrations the Territorials marched back to Westerham. The Territorials and the Cadets also made preparations for their annual summer camps. The Cadets were going to Bexhill and the Territorials to Longmoor Camp in Hampshire, where they would be joined by other units of the Home Counties Brigade.

In early July, the *Westerham Herald* reported the murder of the Austrian Archduke Frans Ferdinand at Sarajevo by Serbian assassins and also that the Westerham cricketers played Sevenoaks (match drawn, G. Streatfield scoring 24). On Saturday 25 July, when the Austrian ultimatum to Serbia expired, the Swan Cinema was showing *Fighters of the Plains*, a Western, together with a drama called the *Lost Heir*. On that afternoon the cricketers played Oxted at Squerryes – an easy win for Westerham (C.N. Watney scored 62) . On Sunday 26th, the Territorials left by train for summer camp and on the 28th Austria declared war on Serbia.

On Thursday 30 July, Russia – as an ally of Serbia – began mobilising its army. Germany sent an ultimatum to Russia to cease mobilising or a state of war would exist between them. In

Hampshire, the Territorials began a route march to Salisbury Plain and in Germany the Imperial Army began mobilising.

In Westerham, Saturday 1 August was the start of the Bank Holiday weekend and various activities were planned. The Cadet Corps held a 'Water Fete' on land adjacent to their headquarters at Verrall's Corner. Events included boating on the Long Pond, various sideshows and a parade of decorated prams and bicycles. The proceedings were opened by the Honourable Mrs Warde – however, a notable absentee was the Cadets' leader, Captain Beresford, who, at the worsening international situation, had been recalled to his Territorial Army unit of the London Regiment. On the Bank Holiday Monday, Westerham's cricketers played Croydon, winning by nine runs.

The August Bank Holiday of 1914 was to mark the passing of the Old World. In the context of prevailing European order, a neighbouring country mobilising her army was tantamount to a declaration of war. The German mobilisation was immediately countered by general mobilisation in France. On Bank Holiday Monday, Germany gave Belgium an ultimatum demanding unrestricted passage for her army to invade France. Throughout the Continent, diplomatic activity reached a frenzy while across Europe, from Moscow to the Pyrenees, millions of men began mustering for duty at army depots and packed troop trains began leaving for prearranged war stations.

On the Tuesday morning, 4 August 1914, as Westerhamers returned to work after the holiday weekend, German troops began crossing into Belgium. The last hope of Britain avoiding a Continental war had gone. As a guarantor of Belgian neutrality Britain was now beyond the brink. In a statement reminiscent of Neville Chamberlain's broadcast in September 1939, the British government demanded the immediate withdrawal of German forces in Belgium by midnight or a state of war would exist. No response was ever received. Great Britain was now at war.

Westerham at War

Those most immediately affected by the declaration of war were the local members of the Territorial Army currently engaged in their annual camp. The beginning of hostilities saw them arriving on Salisbury Plain after a route march across Hampshire from where they were immediately dispatched to prearranged war stations guarding the Kent coast. It would be a long time before any of these men were to change back into civilian clothes. Some would never do so. Others for whom the war had an immediate affect were the men in the Reserves. Men with recent military service typically spent five years on the Reserve List after discharge and were subject to recall in a national emergency. A small number of Westerham men would be the recipients of War Office telegrams instructing them to proceed forthwith to their regimental depots. Some would find themselves rudely shaken out of civilian life and fighting in France within a matter of weeks.

Prior to 1914, a contingency plan already existed whereby in the event of a European war a British Expeditionary Force would be dispatched to the continent to take up position alongside the French Army. The men who began crossing to France in August 1914 were members of Britain's small (by Continental standards) regular army raised without conscription, whose main function was to garrison the far-flung stations of the Empire. These men should not be confused with the civilians who were to step forward in their thousands in response to Lord Kitchener's 'Call to Arms' in the coming months.

The British Expeditionary Force of August 1914 was made up of professional soldiers; men mainly from the lower orders of society who had forsaken the tedium of the factory and farm by signing up for years in uniform and the chance of steady employment, travel and perhaps adventure. They carried with them a lexicon of terminology gained from their postings to exotic locations in various parts of the Empire. A woman was a 'bint' and tea was 'char', washing was 'dhobeying' while an unspecific person was a 'wallah'. Home was 'Blighty', the corruption of another Hindi word, and even the colour of their

11

uniform derived its name from the dust of the Punjab plains – 'khaki'. They were men not overly motivated by patriotism and high ideals, they were just doing their job. They were professionals, noted for their stoicism and their firepower with the Lee Enfield rifle. Twenty-mile route marches, 15 rounds a minute and all for a shilling a day.

Thus in the first weeks of August, units of the British Army began arriving at French Channel ports, moving towards the Belgian border and concentrating near the small mining town of Mons. It was here on 23 August 1914 that the British Expeditionary Force fired their first shots of the War, clashing with the German Army as it swung through Belgium in an attempt to envelop the Allies and encircle Paris. The 1st Battalion, Royal West Kents, were to receive great acclaim for the Battle of Mons where the infantryman's fire power beat off repeated attacks by three battalions of Brandenburg Grenadiers.

The following Westerham men are known to have taken part in the Battle of Mons, the retreat from Mons, the subsequent fighting on the River Aisne and to have been awarded the 1914 (Mons) Star:

Captain Lionel Ashburner, 'Breaches'	4th Battalion Royal Fusiliers,
Private George Alfred Hider, London Road	2nd Battalion Grenadier Guards,
Private William Hayward, Moretons Cottages	Royal Sussex Regiment,
Driver Harry Fenton,	Army Service Corps
Sergeant Henry G. Jupp,	Royal Artillery
Private Arthur P. Newman,	3rd Hussars
Private Harry A. Miles, 'Southview'	Army Ordnance Corps,
Lance Corporal Charles M. Rose, Old Vicarage Cottage	Army Ordnance Corps,
Driver Horace A. Sales, Vicarage Hill	Army Service Corps,

Driver James Utting, Stratton Terrace	Army Service Corps,
Private Walter R. Webb, Duncans Yard	2nd Grenadier Guards,
Private George Munday, Madan Road	1st Battalion Middlesex Regiment,
Private John Yorkston, Madan Road	2nd Battalion Leicestershire Regiment,
Gunner William Blissett, Quebec Cottages	Royal Horse Artillery,

The first named, Captain Ashburner, served with great distinction at the Battle of Mons where he commanded a Company of the 4th Royal Fusiliers in which two men were awarded the Victoria Cross – the first awards of the Great War. Captain Ashburner was wounded at Mons and more seriously wounded again a month later. George Hider and William Hayward were both Reservists recalled to the Colours in August 1914 from their occupations as Westerham postmen. They were to have a bizarre reunion a few weeks later, meeting on the River Aisne after the retreat from Mons. Harry Fenton was another Westerham Reservist hastily recalled to duty from his employment at Mr Evenden's garage. George Munday of the 1st Middlesex was reported wounded by shrapnel on 26 August during the British Army's action at Le Cateau. John Yorkston's battalion, the 2nd Leicesters, was one of a number of units hurriedly brought home from India. Walter Webb, another Westerham postman recalled to duty, was severely wounded within a month of landing in France. The last named, William Blissett, has the melancholy distinction of being Westerham's first casualty of the war.

Yet for the Territorials of the 4th Battalion, Royal West Kents, who were stationed on the Kent coast, 'war service' began to appear as something of a misnomer. Serious as the war situation may have been, it was soon apparent that there was no immediate threat of invasion and hence little for the home-based soldiers to do. By September 1914, however, the Regulars

13

fighting in France were so hard pressed that the Territorials were asked to volunteer for active service. Those who stepped forward together with an influx of new recruits enabled the 4th Royal West Kents to split into Foreign Service and Home Service units. Subsequently these would be known as the 1st/4th and 2nd/4th Battalions, Royal West Kent Regiment. Yet, in the event, the foreign service for which the men had volunteered proved not to be the fighting taking place in France but garrison duty in India. Here they were required to take over from regular army battalions to enable them to be sent to reinforce the Expeditionary Force in France. On 29 October 1914 the 1st/4th Royal West Kents together with the 1st/5th Battalion, kitted out for tropical service, sailed from Southampton on the troopship *Grantully Castle*. Those on board, including many Westerham men, would not see home again for five years. Yet as many of these men would later acknowledge, they would be spared the horrors and rigour of fighting on the Western Front and with a few exceptions would return home at the end of the war.

The following Westerham men are known to have served in India with the 1st/4th Battalion, Royal West Kents:

Charles Adams*	New Street
George Blake*	Madan Road
Walter Bennett	Brewery Cottages
Frederick George Collins*	
Harry Gardiner*	South Bank
Harry English	Mill Street
Daniel Gramson	High Street
Harry Hoath*	High Street
William Hoath	High Street
John Jupp	London Road
Charles W. Lockyer*	French Street
Herbert R. Lockyer*	French Street
Frederick Paige*	Mill Street
Herbert Peters*	High Street
William Newman*	London Road
John Newman*	Palin's Cottages

Edward Newton*	The Green
Leslie Rowe	Squerryes Gardens
Walter Henry Rowe	Squerryes Gardens
George A.S. Selby*	Madan Road
Arthur Streatfield	Mill Cottages
Joseph Smith*	French Street
George E. Stevens*	
Robert G. Stone*	New Street
Charles Laurence Taylor*	High Street
Arthur Bell Townsend*	High Street
George Whitmore	The Crown Hotel
Charles Ward	
Charles Norman Watney	Valence (Lieutenant Colonel in command)
Frederick Whiting*	Madan Road
Edward Wood*	High Street
Percy Wood*	French Street
Leslie Yorkston*	Madan Road

The 1st/4th Royal West Kents landed in India in December 1914 where they first took up garrison duties at Jubbulpore. Over the next five years the battalion was at various stations on the subcontinent from where some younger men were brought home to fight in France and some received promotion into other units. Those who remained with the battalion for the duration eventually went into action in 1919 on the Northwest Frontier in a war against rebel tribesmen. Those whose names are marked * served on the Northwest Frontier and received the India General Service Medal with the clasp 'Afghanistan: Northwest Frontier 1919'.

Garrison Westerham

The speed at which events unfolded over the August Bank Holiday weekend had taken nearly everyone by surprise. When Westerhamers returned to work on Tuesday 4 August 1914, not only were they part of a community on the brink of war, there were already noticeable absentees through men in the Reserves being recalled to duty. As the international crisis deepened over the preceding days, the government had taken the opportunity to mobilise Reservists and place the armed forces on a war footing. People who had ventured away from home over the Bank Holiday looking to use one of the special railway excursions had found most of them cancelled – troop trains were running instead. (This was an age when the railways ran extra trains at holiday weekends instead of closing down the network as is now the norm.) On Tuesday morning, the Westerham post office found itself short of several deliverymen while the brewery was also missing some of its staff. By the end of the week it was clear that the Territorials were not returning from their summer camp. The town would have to manage without a further 60 men of its workforce.

On Wednesday 12 August, a National Service Association held its first meeting at the Drill Hall, Westerham, chaired by the Honourable Mrs Warde. It declared its aims as supporting the servicemen away from home in any way possible and also to include help for their families. A clothing workroom was immediately set up so that useful garments could be made and sent to the troops. A public meeting was also held at the Drill Hall under the title 'Why We Have Gone to War', at which various guest speakers explained the need for the present action. The meeting urged young men with few responsibilities to enlist for the duration of the crisis. A 'Call to Arms' poster was printed in the *Westerham Herald* and a patriotic film entitled *Our Army and Navy* was shown at the Swan Cinema. Special constables were also sworn in at the Drill Hall.

The tensions of the new war situation inevitably sparked a number of spy scares. Cadets at their Headquarters at Verrall's

Corner reported that flashing lights had been seen emanating from woods adjacent to Squerryes Court. On investigation these proved to be the dying embers of an earlier bonfire. Men who had been seen tampering with telephone cables also turned out to be bona fide post office engineers.

There were a number of khaki weddings in the town immediately prior to the Territorials' departure for India. Walter Bennett of Brewery Cottages and Herbert Lockyer of French Street were both married to local girls in ceremonies at St Mary's church. Other military activity was noted when scores of remount horses were driven through Westerham en route to the Artillery Depot at Woolwich. Horses as well as men were being called up for war. Further military movements included a battalion of the Loyal North Lancashire Regiment marching through the town to billets at Oxted, having earlier detrained at Sevenoaks.

On 14 October, the number of uniforms to be seen in the town was further augmented by the establishment of a Red Cross hospital at Dunsdale House on the Brasted Road. Initially many of the wounded cared for by the Royal Army Medical Corps and volunteer staff were Belgian soldiers whose homeland had by then been largely overrun. Some of these expatriate soldiers succumbed to their wounds and were buried in St Mary's churchyard. The National Service Committee and other local bodies were quickly providing blankets, clothing, cigarettes and other comforts for the wounded soldiers at Dunsdale.

Westerham's military status was further increased by the arrival of the 2nd West Lancashire Brigade, Royal Field Artillery. On 22 October several hundred Territorial Army men from Preston, Lancashire, entered the town with their horses, guns, limbers and equipment to be billeted around the district. The artillery lines were established in fields opposite the brewery and the ammunition column was parked below the churchyard. The stay of the 2nd West Lancs. RFA was marked by cordial relationships between the townspeople and the artillerymen. The Men's Club extended honorary membership to all visiting

17

soldiers in uniform and various facilities were placed at the troops' disposal. In return the Lancashire men entered fully into the community with sports matches, displays and musical entertainment. Many of these visiting soldiers maintained links with the town long after they had left for France.

* * *

In the wider theatre it was becoming all too apparent that a manpower crisis was looming. Even with the Reserves mobilised, the troops brought home from India and the deployment of Territorial units, the army in France was almost fighting for its survival. The first Territorial Army battalion to fight in France, the 14th Londons (London Scottish), landed at Le Havre on 16 September 1914 and was quickly followed by many others. Throughout the months of October and November, all available manpower, including Indian troops and Gurkhas, were fed into the maelstrom of the First Battle of Ypres in a desperate action to stop the German advance on the Channel ports. Yet all this was merely to avoid defeat – if the war was to be won the army would need to be vastly expanded.

From the outset, the Secretary of State for War, Lord Kitchener, had reasoned that the conflict would not be quickly resolved. His plans called for the raising of a New Army from scratch that would only take the field when fully trained. Before the end of August 1914, the call had gone out for the 'first hundred thousand' volunteers and this was quickly followed by a second. The stern-faced picture of Lord Kitchener with drooping moustache and brooding eyes, declaring 'Your Country Needs YOU' stared out from billboards and publications everywhere. The response was overwhelming. At recruiting depots all over the country men flocked to volunteer for service. The Royal West Kents alone began forming a 6th, 7th and 8th Battalion and would eventually raise two more.

In the industrial North of England individual towns and districts began raising their own units, the so-called 'Pals' battalions, which were then attached to their local regiments. (The raising of these units exclusively from close-knit communities would later have terrible consequences when they eventually went into action.) Initially all these New Army units were short of all the essentials of war. Uniforms, rifles, accommodation and even officers to lead them were not immediately available, yet whatever the New Armies lacked in equipment they made up for in enthusiasm. However, none of these newly-formed battalions would be ready to take the field before the following year. The army fighting desperately in France would have to hold on as best it could.

Thus in the autumn of 1914, besides the dozen or so Westerham soldiers already at the Front and the Territorials on their way to India, a steady trickle of townsmen began forsaking home and workplace to answer their country's call to arms. Westerham men known to have enlisted in the early months of the war included:

Thomas Butler Bodman	Greencroft	Rifle Brigade
Frederick Yorkston	Madan Road	Rifle Brigade
Henry Singleton	New Street	Royal Field Artillery
David Downs	Valence	Cameron Highlanders
William Martin	Railway Terrace	Royal West Kents
George Harry Fennell	Force Green	Royal West Kents
Fred Ford	Kings Arms	19th Hussars
Sydney Charles King	New Street	The Queen's (RW Surreys)
Joseph Cowell	Quebec Square	Royal West Kents
Arthur Baldry	Pilgrim House School	Royal Army Medical Corps
Albert Newton	The Green	Royal West Kents
Fred Gallup	Madan Road	Royal West Kents

Archibald Ayres	High Street	Royal West Kents
Arthur C Mills	The Green	Royal Garrison Artillery
Sydney Lambert	(former gamekeeper)	Royal West Kents
John Newman	Palin's Cottages	Royal West Kents
Peter Barnett	Palin's Cottages	Royal West Kents
William Jesse Bird	Lodge Lane	Royal West Kents
Henry Whitebread	Church Alley	Army Service Corps
Harry Denis Pennicard	Farley	Army Vetinerary Corps
Horace Wood	French Street	Royal West Kents
Fred Whiting	Madan Road	Royal West Kents

Westerham men enlisting or already serving in other Territorial Army units included:

Douglas W. Genge	Market Square	Honourable Artillery Company
Harold Verrall	The Forge	Honourable Artillery Company
John Thomas Downs	Valence	7th Battalion London Regiment
Fred H.S. Selby	Madan Road	13th Battalion London Regiment

Andrew Downs	Valence	1st London Regiment
Ernest Salmon	London Road	West Kent Yeomanry
Frederick Salmon	London Road	West Kent Yeomanry
Albert Pope	French Street	West Kent Yeomanry
Albert H.O. Streatfeild	Crockham Street	Royal Sussex Regiment

Inevitably, the severity of the fighting taking place at Ypres ensured there was also a steady flow of wounded men in the other direction. The Dunsdale hospital was kept busy with men whose wounds were suitable for immediate repatriation while others more seriously wounded and less able to withstand the journey home remained at base hospitals in France. Some of Westerham's own wounded also came home. Sergeant Munday of Madan Road was wounded by shrapnel in the early fighting. He would return to France after his recovery. Walter Webb of the 2nd Grenadier Guards came home to Duncan's Yard in early November 1914 after suffering severe wounds to the hand and right leg. He was discharged from the army on account of his wounds on 30 November. In late October, news was also received of Westerham's first fatality of the Great War.

Gunner William Blisset, Royal Horse Artillery

William Blissett, of 5 Quebec Cottages, Westerham, was among the Reservists recalled to duty at the outbreak of war. Born in Westerham in 1891, he was the second son of Henry and Sarah Blissett. He attended Hosey School and subsequently worked as a post office messenger. He later enlisted in the army where he served in the Royal Horse Artillery before being discharged to the Reserve in January 1914. Just six months after resuming his work

21

with the post office he was recalled to the army and landed in France with the 7th Brigade, Royal Horse Artillery, on 15 August 1914. Blissett was in action at the Battles of Mons and Le Cateau and after the long retreat from Mons was again involved in the fighting on the River Aisne. Here the war of movement had ended with both sides digging in – the beginning of trench warfare. Gunner Blissett died on 28 September 1914 aged 24, from causes undisclosed at the time. William Blissett was killed accidentally. William Blissett is buried at Villers-en-Prayeres, Aisne, France.

As Christmas 1914 approached, an appeal was made for various comforts in the form of cigarettes, chocolate and clothing to be handed in at the vicarage for onward dispatch to local men serving away from home. Many of the gifts were sent on to the Territorials of the 1st/4th Royal West Kents who arrived in India on 2 December. The National Service Committee continued to dispatch useful clothing to men at the Front and a concert at the Men's Club raised £20 for the War Fund. An appeal was also made from Buckingham Palace for Princess Mary's Sailors and Soldiers Christmas Gift Fund. Donations were invited to enable a small tin of cigarettes and tobacco to be sent to each serviceman on Christmas Day. (Thousands of these small embossed tins were distributed, many of which survive to this day to be seen among antiques and curios.) On Christmas Day the locally billeted troops paraded at St Mary's church for a Christmas service, and gifts for the wounded soldiers were handed in at the Dunsdale Hospital. As the year ended prayers were offered for an early end to the war.

1915

The beginning of 1915 saw the soldiers serving in France become part of a new subterranean world. As the fighting subsided with the onset of winter, the armies had dug in where they stood. On Christmas Day 1914, there had been an outbreak of fraternisation among the opposing troops in some sectors. Commanding officers had excused this behaviour by taking the opportunity to observe enemy defences and to recover the dead of earlier fighting.

By the New Year, the front line stretched like an open scar across the face of Europe. Beginning on the Belgian coast at Nieuport, it ran across Flanders and the French industrial areas of Lens and Bethune, then south through the chalk downland of the Somme region and on to the wooded slopes above the Rivers Aisne and Marne before ending among the Vosges Mountains at the Swiss border. In all there existed some 400 miles of trenches, earthworks and redoubts in which the opposing armies lived and confronted each other in mutual cold, wet, discomfort and danger.

For the British manning the northern sector around Ypres and the French border the conditions were among the worst. Here the low-lying land and recovered polder was often flooded and any digging activity encountered water within a few feet of the surface. Water and mud accumulated in the trenches to freeze by night and return to slime by day. Where duckboards had not been introduced to raise the bottom of the trenches, men stood in mud and water, causing many soldiers to be invalided with a new disease of trench foot. The permanence of the trench system was also emphasised by the names often applied to individual trenches by the inhabiting soldiers. 'Piccadilly' and 'Regent Street' were commonplace names for trenches manned by London Regiments while 'Argyle Street' and 'Princes Street' denoted those occupied by Highlanders.

Besides the general discomfort there was also continual danger from enemy action. In all sectors snipers were active and the daily routine was often interspersed with mutual bomb-throwing and mortar bombardments. Reliefs and the bringing up of rations were usually restricted to periods of darkness and were not easily accomplished. Turns at the front line represented the greatest danger to the soldiers, but even in the rear there was a constant risk of random enemy shelling.

Typically, an infantry battalion would enter the trenches for three days at the front-line, with three days in support followed by a period in reserve, after which the battalion would be withdrawn to its divisional area for rest, training and 'working fatigues'.

The winter campaign of 1915 was conducted without any major Allied offensive. The Germans, who occupied a vast swathe of territory, were also content to remain on the defensive. Yet even in these so-called 'quiet periods', the casualties in the British Army alone often ran into thousands a day. The British and French generals who wrestled with the problem of breaking the trench deadlock and ousting the invader could only wait for the spring and for the arrival of more troops.

Meanwhile the soldiers in the front line endured unremitting hardship and danger. By day they would 'stand to' at dawn, provide sentries, distribute rations, carry out trench repairs, check their weapons and, in a small relief from the daily rigour, enjoy a ration of rum. By night, in a state of heightened vigilance, patrols would enter no man's land, wiring parties repaired the barbed wire defences, supplies were brought up and reliefs made. At all times a constant alert was maintained against the threat of enemy raids. On the night of 25 January 1915, this threat would become a desperate reality for the men of the 1st Battalion, Scots Guards, manning the trenches at Cuinchy, near Bethune, France.

2nd Lieutenant Arthur Horace Lang, 2nd Battalion, Grenadier Guards

Arthur Horace Lang was born on 25 October, 1890. His mother, Mrs Alice Lang, was a daughter of the Haggard family of 'Breaches', Vicarage Hill, Westerham, where she lived for some time during the war years. Arthur Horace Lang was educated at Harrow School and Cambridge University where he excelled at sports. He gained a commission in the Grenadier Guards, Special Reserve, in August 1910 and was mobilised at the outbreak of war. Lang served in France with the 2nd Grenadiers from 29 December 1914 and in January 1915 was attached to the 1st Scots Guards of the same Brigade. It was not unusual for officers to serve with other units within the Guards Brigade; the war diary of 1st Scots Guards simply records that they 'borrowed him'.

On 23 January 1915, the Scots Guards took over the trenches at Cuinchy at a point where the opposing lines were scarcely 25 yards apart. On the night of 24th/25th, a German deserter gave warning of an impending attack on the Guards' front which, after an intense bombardment, proved to be all too true. The Germans rushed the Guards' positions in overwhelming strength, bombing and firing down into their trenches. Although a counter-attack was later mounted, the night's action was a catastrophe for the Scots Guards. Over 150 officers and men were killed and wounded and a further 240 were listed as missing, many of whom were never heard of again.

2nd Lieutenant Lang was among those missing after the attack. Among the papers relating to this young officer, held at the National Archives, are a number of letters from wounded officers and from PoWs in Germany from whom any information on the fate of Lang had been requested. One letter states that he was 'seen to fall', indicating that he was most probably killed in the action.

This part of the front line was not captured from the Germans until April 1917, when presumably his body was found. One report states that he was identified by his cap badge (no doubt, a lone Grenadier among the fallen Scots Guards). Arthur Horace Lang is now buried in the Canadian Cemetery at Neuville St Vast, France.

Westerham 1915

At the beginning of 1915, whatever feelings existed about the war amongst Westerham citizens, one thing at least was abundantly clear. The hopes of an early end to the fighting and the troops marching home had now evaporated. Any initial enthusiasm and thoughts of a quick victory had disappeared to be replaced by a growing realisation that perhaps a far greater struggle would ensue than had been first envisaged. An ominous development was the report of an airship raid on Great Yarmouth on 20 January. Otherwise, life in the town carried on as normally as possible in the circumstances. The various clubs and organisations held their AGMs: the Gardeners' Club met at the King's Arms and the Men's Club at the clubhouse. At the latter event, 60 soldiers from the locally billeted units were invited. The meeting was followed by a 'smoking concert' in which attendees gave recitals, musical solos and vocals. In an age before radio and television there was no shortage of talent among the locals and visiting troops – a fine evening's entertainment was reported.

The National Service Committee opened a lending library at the Drill Hall to raise funds to support the men away from home and regular donations of clothing and foodstuffs were made to the wounded soldiers at the Dunsdale Hopital. The Swan Cinema also kept up a good variety of films.

A significant improvement to the facilities available to visiting troops and townspeople was the opening of St Mary's Hall in the London Road. The hall served as a canteen for the troops stationed in the district and as a venue for dances and concerts held by local organisations. The opening ceremony was performed by the Reverend Le Mesurier on Sunday 15 February before an assembled crowd and the hall was immediately the centre for many activities.

In early 1915, men were still being exhorted to enlist in the army and the appeals to patriotism still produced a steady flow of recruits. Perhaps surprisingly, this call to arms had also been enthusiastically met in other parts of the world, most notably in the Dominions of the British Empire. In Canada and Australia

27

such numbers had stepped forward to enlist that armies representative of their own nations were being formed. Among the volunteers of the new Dominion forces were many young men who had earlier left Britain to seek their fortunes in the New World. Now in a continuation of their quest for adventure or in a desire to come to the aid of the old country (and sometimes both), these men began returning to Britain as soldiers of the Canadian Expeditionary Force and the Australian Imperial Force. At least eight former Westerham men served in the Dominion Forces during the war, including Christopher Pickett of Railway Terrace, Wallace Pritchard of Aberdeen House, Nathan Salmon of Grange Cottages, Charles Fisk of High Street, Frank Ernest Clarke, William Friend and Albert Watts. Four of these expatriate servicemen are listed on the Westerham war memorial – among them John William Penfold, formerly of Quebec Square.

Private John William Penfold, 13th Battalion, Canadian Infantry

John William Penfold was born at Westerham on 18 January 1879, the son of John and Annie Penfold of 10 Quebec Cottages. He attended Hosey School and as a young man was also a member of the local Volunteer Battalion, Royal West Kent Regiment. On 8 August 1898 he enlisted in the Royal Field Artillery at Shorncliffe where his previous occupation was stated as a 'labourer'. He served in South Africa from the outbreak of the Boer War in 1899 and was wounded (accidentally) with a gunshot wound to the hand. He returned to England in 1900 and was discharged from the army in 1901 with poor health, having been awarded the Queen's South Africa Medal. Penfold subsequently lived in Reading, where he married, before emigrating to Canada. In 1914 he was living in Water Street, West Brockville, Ontario. At the outbreak of war he again enlisted, this time in the Canadian Forces and in early 1915 he was part of the first Canadian contingent to arrive in Britain. Soon after landing, however, he was admitted to the Brompton Hospital with a respiratory disease. When the disease proved to be incurable, he was allowed home to his parents, then living at 9 Railway Terrace, Westerham. John Penfold died at Westerham on 18 February 1915, aged 36. On Wednesday 24 February, his body was borne on a gun carriage of the 2nd West Lancashire Field Artillery from Railway Terrace to the parish church. There, following a full military funeral conducted by the Reverend Le Mesurier and the sounding of the 'Last Post' by regimental trumpeters, he was laid to rest in St Mary's churchyard. His grave, marked by a war graves headstone, can be found near the footpath leading to Quebec Avenue.

The end of winter 1915 saw little change in the deadlocked trench warfare on the Western Front. The British had attacked at Neuve Chappelle in March and again in May at Aubers Ridge. The Germans had also carried out an attack in April on the Ypres sector introducing the new dimension of poisoned gas to the horrors to be endured by the soldiers. In all cases the attacks had largely broken down, with limited territorial gains and mounting casualties. Just south of Ypres, there was vicious fighting during April and May for control of Hill 60. Despite its imposing name the hill was no more than the spoil heap of a railway cutting designated by its height above sea level. Sergeant George Munday of the Middlesex Regiment from Madan Road was wounded again in the Hill 60 fighting, with a bullet wound to the chest.

May in Westerham saw the departure of the 2nd West Lancashire Brigade, Royal Field Artillery. Their stay in the town of nearly seven months had been marked by good relationships and much cordiality. On Sunday 22 May, a large crowd assembled in the market square to see the Gunners march off, led by their commanding officer, Colonel Ryland. They were to land in France in September. The fortunes and exploits, and the casualties, of the 2nd West Lancs were faithfully reported in the *Westerham Herald* throughout the war.

All over England in the summer of 1915 the scenes at Westerham were repeated in hundreds of other towns and villages. Battalions, brigades and divisions of Kitchener's New Army were beginning to move towards France. After months of formation, organising, equipment and training, these new and untried units were now deemed to be ready for war. The newly-formed 6th Battalion, Royal West Kent Regiment, landed in France on 1 June, and was quickly followed by the 7th Battalion in July and the 8th Battalion in August.

The ranks of the 2nd/4th Battalion Royal West Kent, stationed at Canterbury, in which many Westerham Territorials were serving, had been swelled by recruitment to the point where it again split into 'home' and 'foreign service' components. The home service unit was subsequently designated as the 3rd/4th Battalion while the 2nd/4th was placed on a war footing and prepared for overseas service.

Two further New Army units, in which Westerham men were serving, also landed in France in the early summer of 1915. These were the 6th Battalion, the Buffs (East Kent Regiment) on 2 June, and on 15 May, the 7th Battalion, Rifle Brigade.

Lance Corporal Thomas Butler Bodman, 7th Battalion, Rifle Brigade

Thomas Butler Bodman was the son of Thomas and Martha Bodman of Greencroft, Farley Common. Although originally from Calne in Wiltshire, by 1901 the family was resident in Westerham where Thomas worked as a groom. Young Thomas attended Hosey School and was also a member of the Westerham Cadet Corps. Prior to the First World War he also served in the Volunteer Battalion of the Royal West Kents. At the outbreak of war he enlisted in the Rifle Brigade at Winchester and was posted to the 7th Battalion, which was one of the many

New Army units then being raised throughout the country. After formation and training, the Battalion was assigned to the 41st Infantry Brigade of the 14th Division. As part of the build up of the British forces in France, Thomas Bodman and the 7th Rifle Brigade crossed to France on 19 May 1915. Throughout May and June the battalion took turns in the trenches at Ypres, mainly by companies and under the instruction of experienced units.

On 22 July, the 7th Rifle Brigade relieved the Gordon Highlanders at Hooge, a small and largely devastated village a few miles south east of Ypres along the Menin Road. The Hooge sector was the scene of severe local battles and mining activity, with opposing forces tunnelling under each other's defences before placing explosives, which were then detonated to the accompaniment of all-out attacks. This was the fate of the 7th Rifle Brigade on 24 July when a mine was exploded under their trenches. In the attack that followed the Germans introduced the new horror of flamethrowers, jetting streams of burning liquid into the British trenches. A few days later, the 7th Rifle Brigade were part of a counter-attack to retrieve the lost ground. In this disastrous action over 300 men were listed as killed, wounded or missing. Private Bodman is deemed to have been killed in action on this day, 30 July 1915. His body was never found and his name is now recorded on the Menin Gate Memorial, Ypres, Belgium. Thomas Butler Bodman was 23 and had been in France for ten weeks.

Lieutenant James Gordon Hamilton Greig, 6th Battalion East Kent Regiment

On a small side road leading from Westerham Hill, less than two miles north of the town, stands an imposing house called 'The Mount'. In 1914 this was the home of John Charles Hamilton Greig, who was the managing director of the William Cory Shipping Company. William Corys owned a large fleet of colliers and other coasters, and also distributed coal and oil throughout London and the south-east. The son of John Charles Hamilton Greig was born at Welling, Kent on 27 April 1895 and was educated at Glenalmond School. In August 1914, young James, then aged 19, enlisted in the 5th Battalion, Royal Sussex Regiment. He was very quickly selected for a commission and became a 2nd Lieutenant in the 6th Battalion, East Kent Regiment on 19 September 1914.

The 6th East Kents, a New Army battalion, began forming at Colchester in September 1914 from the men who had stepped forward to answer Lord Kitchener's call to arms. Among the 6th East Kents were several hundred men from the firm of William Cory who formed D Company and were also known as 'Cory's Company'. On his appointment to the 6th East Kents, 2nd Lieutenant Hamilton Greig joined D Company to find himself among his father's old employees. (William Corys were to be a paternal support to their enlisted employees and dependants in the years ahead.) The battalion moved to Shorncliffe in November 1914 and was eventually brigaded with the 6th Royal West Kents and two other newly-raised battalions from the Queen's Regiment and the East Surreys. They embarked for France on 2 June 1915.

Soon after landing the 6th East Kents moved to the front line near Armentieres to begin a period of induction in trench warfare, which was followed in July by turns in the trenches near the Belgian border at Ploegsteert. The History of the Buffs (East Kent Regiment) describes August 1915 as a quiet period for the 6th Battalion, however, during this time of routine trench warfare, 2nd Lieutenant Hamilton Greig aged 20, was mortally wounded. On the night of 8 August he was leading a party of men repairing barbed wire defences in no man's land, when he was hit. He succumbed to his wounds on 13 August and was buried at Bailleul, France.

In July 1915, the 2nd/4th Battalion, Royal West Kent was among the many army units to receive orders for overseas service. After its formation in May of the same year, the Battalion had spent two months of intensive training at Bedford but with the arrival of embarkation orders came the issue of tropical clothing. It was clear that France would not be their destination. On 20 July the Battalion sailed from Devonport in the troopship *Northland* arriving 11 days later at Alexandria in Egypt. From there they sailed to Mudros in the Aegean as a last stop before landing to reinforce the Mediterranean Expeditionary Force on the rocky shores of the Gallipoli peninsula.

The Gallipoli campaign had opened in early 1915 as a way of bypassing the apparent stalemate then prevailing on the Western Front and as a means of attacking Turkey who had entered the war on the side of Germany in November 1914. The object of the campaign was to eliminate Turkey from the war, and also to open a supply route to Russia via the Dardanelles waterway, which linked the Mediterranean with the Black Sea. Initially, the Royal Navy had attempted to force the Dardanelles using warships alone, but when this had failed a combined French and British amphibious assault was carried out on the Gallipoli peninsula at the southern end of the Narrows. The Gallipoli campaign was to see the first deployment of the newly-raised Australian Imperial Force and New Zealand Expeditionary Force. The combined Australian and New Zealand Army Corps had moved to Egypt in early 1915 and had then taken part in the initial landings on 25 April 1915. This day has ever after been commemorated in the Southern Hemisphere as 'ANZAC Day'.

Among the Australians who fought at Gallipoli were several young men originally from Westerham: including Christopher Pickett from Railway Terrace, Charles Fisk from High Street and Nathan George Salmon of Grange Cottages, London Road.

Gunner Nathan George Salmon, 3rd Brigade, Australian Field Artillery

Nathan George Salmon was the son of Perridge and Caroline Salmon of Grange Cottages, London Road, Westerham. In 1914 Perridge Salmon was a well-known Westerham builder and contractor. Nathan Salmon, who was the second of four sons, attended Hosey School and was also a member of the Westerham Cadet Corps. He was among many young men of his time who left home to seek their fortunes in the New World and was living in Australia at the outbreak of war. He enlisted in 1914 and served with Australian Field Artillery.

On the first day of the Gallipoli landings the Australians and New Zealanders landed at the beachhead on the west coast of the peninsula that was ever after known as 'ANZAC Beach'. Here the Australians were locked in close-quarter fighting with the Turks for many months. The campaign reached a climax in August 1915 when simultaneous attacks were made on all fronts together with further landings at Suvla Bay just north of ANZAC Beach. Nathan George Salmon was killed in action during this period of intense fighting on 25 August. He was buried at Shell Green Cemetery near to the furthest point of advance of the Australian beachhead.

The 2nd/4th Battalion Royal West Kents meanwhile had landed at Gallipoli on 10 August 1915. They came ashore as reinforcements to the Suvla Bay landings, which had taken place just two days earlier. Yet already the surprise and impetus of the initial landings had been lost and the West Kents found themselves digging in close to the beach. The newly-arrived Territorials had to quickly adapt themselves to trench warfare with persistent shelling and sniping and to a steady drain of casualties, many due to sickness. In the coming weeks the battalion alternated with turns in the front line and periods in reserve near the beach. At all times there was constant discomfort and danger from random shelling.

October saw the arrival of more Westerham men on the peninsula with the landing of the West Kent Yeomanry. The Yeomanry were the cavalry arm of the Territorial Army, also manned by volunteers, who in more leisurely times were required to provide their own horses. This tended to make the Yeomanry units the preserve of the landed classes, but in 1914 recruiting was thrown open to all who would join and who were willing to learn horsemanship. In the event however, the Yeomanry companies who landed at Gallipoli were without their horses and were employed as infantry in the front line. Among the West Kent Yeomanry troops who landed at Helles in early October were Ernest and Frederick Salmon of Grange Cottages, Westerham. (One can only wonder whether these two men could have been aware that their elder brother Nathan had been killed in the fighting a few miles away just six weeks earlier.) Ernest was later wounded at Gallipoli.

With the approach of winter, it became clear to the Allies that no progress could be achieved at Gallipoli, far less the objectives of the campaign. With battlefield stalemate and mounting casualties, many from dysentery, the decision was taken to evacuate the peninsula. By the end of 1915 the campaign was closed down with little to show for all the effort, expenditure, heroism and over 30,000 Allied dead.

Westerham men who served with the 2nd/4th Royal West Kents at Gallipoli include:

Sergeant Major Thomas Henry Martle, Westerham Territorials instructor, invalided home and later discharged
Private Alfred (Jimmy) Allen, Invalided home and later wounded in France
Private Albert W. Wood, Later wounded in France
Private Frederick Gallop, Later wounded in France
Private Frederick Grimes, Killed in action on 16 August 1915

Fred Grimes worked for many years before the war at Mill's bakeries on The Green.

* * *

In Westerham, the first anniversary of the start of the war passed largely unnoticed. The town was still full of uniforms, the 2nd West Lancashires having been replaced by the 2nd/1st Home Counties, Royal Field Artillery as the brigade billeted in the town. The Dunsdale Hospital was still kept busy by a steady flow of wounded from the Front and townspeople rallied to appeals for foodstuffs, clothing and other comforts for the recovering soldiers. The Cadet Corps ran a daily duty rota of orderlies to assist the medical staff and the produce collected for St Mary's church harvest festival was also donated to the hospital. On 29 September, eight more wounded were received at Dunsdale.

The National Service Committee workroom continued to send socks, gloves, mufflers and other items of clothing to men at the Front and concerts and dances were held at St Mary's Hall, often given by the troops stationed in the district. A small-bore rifle range was opened in Squerryes Park, which was used by the Cadets and a local rifle club. October 1915 saw more Westerham men volunteering for the army. Postman Fred Lurcook enlisted in the Royal Engineers along with Frank Jarrett of London Road, who formerly worked for Horton's coal merchants. Arthur Bond of Delegarde Farm joined the Royal Artillery.

In France the build up of New Army divisions went on remorselessly. By September it was considered that sufficient reinforcements were now available to justify a major attack on the Germans with a real chance of success. This offensive would include many units newly-arrived from England who had scarcely had time to adapt to war service. Some would be committed to the attack on their first day at the Front.

One of the infantry divisions of Lord Kitchener's army earmarked for the coming battle was the 15th Scottish, in which two Westerham men were serving. The area chosen for the planned offensive was the small mining town of Loos in the industrial belt of northern France.

Lieutenant John Alfred Pigou Inglis, 73rd Field Company, Royal Engineers

An infantry division of the British Army consisted of 12 infantry battalions organised into three brigades, each of four battalions. The division also included a brigade of field artillery and three companies of Royal Engineers. The Engineers' role was to maintain the communications, transport, defensive earthworks and all the other varied mechanical requirements of the division, which totalled around 15,000 men. The 15th Scottish Division consisted of newly-raised battalions from nearly all the famous Scottish regiments including the Royal Scots, the King's Own Scottish Borderers, the Cameron Highlanders, the Seaforths and the Black Watch.

Serving in one of the attached engineer companies, the 73rd, was Lieutenant Inglis, Royal Engineers, whose parents lived at 'The Nest', French Street, Westerham. Lieutenant Inglis was also the grandson of the distinguished soldier, Major General Sir John Inglis KCB. John Alfred Pigou Inglis was educated at Rugby School before entering the army at the Royal Military Academy, Woolwich, where he excelled at sports, representing the Academy in athletics. He received a commission into the Royal Engineers in April 1914.

The 15th Scottish Division began assembling on Salisbury Plain in the summer of 1915 before crossing to France in mid-July. After periods in the front line for induction in trench warfare, the Division moved to the Bethune area in early September to prepare for the coming battle. The initial attack would be carried out by four infantry divisions and would involve the first employment of poisoned gas by the British Army. The attack was preceded by an artillery bombardment lasting four days.

At 6.30 on the morning of 25 September 1915 the assaulting troops rose from their trenches. On this day the Royal Engineers were detailed to fight as infantry, two sections of the 73rd Field Company REs, led by Lieutenant Inglis, set off in support of the Black Watch and Seaforth Highlanders towards the German strongpoint of Hill 70. The war diary of the 73rd Field Company records that 'almost immediately Lt. Inglis was killed by a shell, the command devolving to a sergeant'. The Engineers pressed on through the town of Loos where they assisted the infantry in consolidating the new position until relieved the following day. The casualties of 73rd Field Company totalled 52 men killed, wounded and missing. Lieutenant Inglis was later buried at the military cemetery, Marzingarbe, France.

Despite some initial success on the first day, the battle was to stall with some lodgements of British troops remaining in the enemy lines. When a further assault was ordered for the following day there would be disastrous consequences for the attacking troops, which would include a further Westerham soldier.

Captain Ian Campbell Penney, 13th Battalion, The Royal Scots

Ian Campbell Penney was born on 1 February 1885, the eldest son of William and Jemima Penney of 'The Knoll', Westerham. 'The Knoll' was a house situated just off the London Road at the approaches to Court Lodge Farm. Ian Campbell Penney, who was educated at Glenalmond School, served in the 13th Royal Scots, one of the newly-raised battalions of the 15th Scottish Division. Captain Penney had been a mining engineer before the war working in Tasmania and Nigeria. Being home on leave when war was declared, he had immediately enlisted. After formation and training, the 13th Royal Scots landed at Boulogne on 10 July 1915. Following a period of training in trench warfare the battalion moved to the

Lens-Bethune area in September to prepare for the coming Battle of Loos. On 25 September the 13th Royal Scots were part of the main assault on the German lines. Attacking with the 15th Scottish Division, they successfully stormed into the town of Loos and on towards the slopes of Hill 70. Despite mounting casualties, the Scots pressed on only to meet with stiffening enemy resistance. By the end of the day, the Scots on Hill 70 were forced to dig in on the reverse slope.

The news of the breaking of the German line emboldened the British command to believe that there was now a gap in the enemy lines that could be exploited. The attack was ordered to be resumed on the following day. Yet on the morning of the 26th, the depleted and exhausted Scots were in no state to continue and any gap in the German lines that may have existed the previous day had now been filled. The assault of 26 September was a catastrophe for the attacking troops. The war diary of the 13th Royal Scots on the 26th states that at 10.30 a.m. troops were seen abandoning Bois Hugo on the flank of Hill 70 and that 'Captain Penney at once led a platoon forward to make good the post vacated, but was shot dead'.

The battle was to drag on for a further two weeks when with limited gains and mounting casualties the inevitable stalemate was accepted. The body of Ian Campbell Penney was never recovered. His name is now listed on the Loos Memorial which stands on the battlefield and records the names of a further 20,000 men who died in the vicinity of Loos and who have no known grave.

Ships Master Ambrose Langley Hunt, SS *Burrsfield*

As the fighting at Loos subsided and the onset of winter called a halt to offensive operations, the war also made melancholy progress in other theatres. The Gallipoli campaign had also stalled after the August attacks and, with little chance of any real breakthrough, plans were brought forward for an evacuation of the peninsula. Yet the troops already ashore still had to be supplied which meant that a colossal amount of shipping was pressed into service running to and fro across the Mediterranean with tons of stores, munitions and all the other needs of an army. This fleet of shipping included a vessel owned by Messrs Taylor, Wood and Brown of London, the SS *Burrsfield*. Built for the coastal coal trade in 1902, the *Burrsfield*, of 4,000 tons, was now carrying war stores between Malta and the Gallipoli expedition base at Mudros in the Aegean.

The Master of the *Burrsfield* was 46-year-old Ambrose Langley Hunt, who was the son of Ambrose Hunt MD of Dungarvon, County Waterford, Ireland. Ambrose Langley Hunt was a professional seagoing officer in the Merchant Navy who had risen to the rank of Ships Master and had earlier served as an officer in the Royal Naval Reserve. On 5 October 1915 the *Burrsfield* was west of Cape Matapan on passage to Mudros when the German submarine U33 intercepted her. In the ensuing gun action the *Burrsfield* was sunk and four of her crew including the Master were killed by shellfire. Ambrose Langley Hunt, who was the husband of Catherine Hunt of Old Hill House, Westerham, is commemorated on the Tower Hill Memorial, London, which lists the names of those members of the Merchant Navy who died at sea in the two world wars.

As Christmas approached, appeals again went out from the Westerham vicarage for gifts and other comforts to be collected and sent to local men serving at the Front. Money was collected for the West Kents in India as the passage time for parcels was considered too great. Plans were made to entertain the troops who would be remaining in the town over Christmas with a concert at St Mary's Hall on Boxing Day. The parish church choir was out carol singing around the town on Christmas Eve with the proceeds of the collection being donated to servicemen blinded in the recent fighting, and on Christmas Day itself there was a parade and church service, which the visiting troops attended. Mr Boddy's butcher shop announced that there would be a good supply of meat and poultry for the festive season and Mr Taylor advertised that his shop in the High Street now had copies of the new music hall song that had suddenly gained great popularity and seemed to capture the mood of the second wartime Christmas. It began:

Keep the home fires burning
While your hearts are yearning
Though your lads are far away
They dream of home.

The lyrics, from a new West End show, perhaps reflected what people were thinking. Yet the following lines talked of silver linings that were little in evidence and who could guess how long it would be before the boys came home?

Keep The Home Fires Burning
Words by Lene Guilbert Ford
Music by Ivor Novello
© 1914 Ascherberg, Hopwood & Crew
Administered by Warner/Chappell Music Ltd, London W6 8BS
Reproduced by permission. All rights Reserved.

1916

In January 1916 an end to the war seemed as far away as ever. Despite all the effort and sacrifice to date, the deadlock appeared as immovable as at the beginning of 1915. The Gallipoli expedition, launched to bypass the Western Front and remove Turkey from the war, had been tried and failed. By 9 January the last troops on the peninsula had slipped away by sea, largely undetected by the Turks. To the generals and politicians there seemed to be no other recourse than to wait for the spring and the arrival of yet more troops. More of Lord Kitchener's New Army divisions were preparing and would soon be landing in France. Then with more guns, more shells and more men, surely the long-awaited breakthrough would be achieved.

For the men of the 1st Battalion, Royal West Kents, Christmas and New Year were spent in the trenches at Carnoy in Picardy where the British had recently taken over a large section of line from the French. There had been no repeat of the previous year's Christmas truce, and the West Kents had even carried out a raid on the opposing German trenches on Boxing Day. After leaving the front line on 6 January, the battalion spent a month in rest and training, which included time for rugby and football matches.

At home, the beginning of 1916 saw a change of status in all potential recruits for the services. Despite the massive response to the earlier call to arms, the army still needed more men. However, by the end of 1915 the number of men volunteering was dwindling. As a first move towards conscription, the Lord Derby Act of 1915 required all men of military age to register and to state their occupation. Initially married men and workers in key industries were exempted but by January 1916 all were included under the Military Service Act. Then it was no longer possible to volunteer and men were simply called up for the army as and when required.

The Act also changed the status of the Territorials who remained at home. Now they were no longer a purely home defence force and the units to which they belonged became liable for service overseas. A system of appeals tribunals were set up to review objections by those conscripted. Appeals could be lodged on the grounds of health, hardship or being a key worker in a business that would otherwise suffer. Tribunals sat in Oxted and Sevenoaks to consider the appeals of men from Westerham and surrounding districts. In most cases successful appeals would only result in enlistment being deferred for a limited period.

In an exception to the new conscription law, the Royal Navy was allowed first call on any man who volunteered for the 'senior service'. The navy, with a much smaller manpower requirement than the army, thus had the pick of the recruits and was largely able to maintain an all-volunteer service throughout the war.

For no matter how unprepared the army may have been for the war of 1914–1918, the same could not be said of the navy. Britain's dependance on seaborne trade, its island status and worldwide Empire all ensured that not even the most naive of politicians would neglect the fleet. Indeed, under the direction of inspirational leaders like Admiral Jackie Fisher, the Royal Navy not only surpassed all other navies in size but in much technical innovation as well. When, in the years preceding the war, Imperial Germany had begun building her own fleet of battleships, the response had been to build 'two for one,' and this was largely achieved.

When war was declared in August 1914, the navy had just completed its 'annual muster' when all ships were fully mobilised and Reservists attended. From there it was a simple step to send the fleet to its prearranged war stations. For the majority of the navy's big gun battleships this was the great fleet anchorage at Scapa Flow in the Orkneys, where it stood guard over the exit from the North Sea into the Atlantic.

Although, in 1914, there were distant German squadrons to be hunted down, for the greater part of the war the British fleet remained at Scapa Flow keeping watch on the German fleet, which seldom ventured from its Wilhelmshaven base on the other side of the North Sea.

Although never in the proportions of those who joined the army, Westerham men were still well represented among those who served at sea. The following list is of men of the town who are known to have served in the Royal Navy between the years 1914 and 1918, many of whom had already enlisted prior to the outbreak of war.

Lieutenant Philip H. Bonham Carter, Submarine C19
George Thos. Gardiner, HMS *Beagle*
Engineer Lieutenant T. Gurnell, HMS *Christopher*
George C. Spillar, HMS *Lord Nelson*
William Bashford, HMS *Cornwallis*
Sidney Watts, HMS *Nimrod*
Lieutenant Leonard Newton, HMS *Orion*
Wallace Wade, HMS *Caradoc*
Albert Singleton, HMS *Suffolk*
George Heath, HMS *Natal*
William J. Singleton, Royal Marines, HMS *Constance*
Frederick W. Hoath, Royal Marines, HMS *Phaeton*

George Heath of Railway Terrace served over 25 years in the navy, ending his service as a Chief Petty Officer. He was a survivor of HMS *Natal*, which sank following an internal explosion at Cromarty, Scotland, in December 1915. Albert Singleton of New Street and Wallace Wade of Brewery Cottages both enlisted as Boy Seamen in the course of the war. Westerham's Royal Marines, William Singleton of New Street and Fred Hoath of Southbank, served with distinction throughout the war years. William Singleton landed in France in September 1914 with the Royal Naval Division, which attempted to hold the port of Dunkirk against the German advance. He also fought with the RN Division at Gallipoli where he was wounded on 27 July 1915. Fred Hoath took part in the famous St George's Day raid on Zeebrugge in April 1918, where he received a mention in despatches. In 1916, both men were serving in ships of the Grand Fleet.

Two more young Westerham men were to enlist in the Royal Navy during the early part of the war and would serve in brief and similarly tragic circumstances.

Ordinary Seaman George Obed Wood, HMS *Turbulent*

For almost the first two years of the war, the British fleet stationed at Scapa Flow saw little or no action. There were occasional alarms when the fleet put to sea, most notably when enemy battleships had crossed the North Sea to shell towns like Whitby and Scarborough, but at the approach of British forces the raiders had always fled. The battle-cruiser squadron had been in action at the Dogger Bank in 1915 in a running battle with its German counterpart, which resulted in German losses and serious damage to some British ships. Yet, for the most part, the British fleet remained at its northern anchorage at immediate readiness.

All this was to change on 30 May 1916 when intelligence reports indicated that the German High Seas Fleet was preparing to sail. During the night of 30 May the British battleships began slipping their moorings. *Agincourt, Marlborough, Thunderer, Conquerer, Iron Duke, Revenge* – ships with names that resound with British history – one by one began passing the harbour mouth and heading for the open sea. By the morning of 31 May the Grand Fleet of 28 battleships, nine battle-cruisers and a host of attendant cruisers and destroyers were thundering out into the North Sea. Among the escorting ships of the 10th Flotilla was the brand-new destroyer HMS *Turbulent*, fresh from her builders on the Tyne, and serving in *Turbulent* in only his third week at sea was George Obed Wood of Westerham.

George Obed Wood was born at Westerham on 1 April 1894. He was the son of Mr and Mrs George Wood, but after the death of his parents he lived with relatives at Park Cottages, near to the entrance to Squerryes Court. He attended Hosey School and later worked as a gardener at Darenth Nurseries. He enlisted in the Royal Navy at Chatham in November 1915. After training at Chatham, George was drafted to HMS *Turbulent*, joining the ship on 12 May 1916.

The Battle of Jutland that took place on the afternoon of 31 May 1916 was to be the world's greatest clash of 'iron clad' warships. The battle was inconclusive in its outcome but by the evening of the 31st the German fleet was retreating. The British remained in pursuit in the hope of forcing a decisive battle on the following day. The fleets were to clash again during the hours of darkness in a confused night action.

Shortly after midnight, *Turbulent*, in company with destroyers of the 13th Flotilla, blundered into the path of the retiring German battleships. In a mêlée of shellfire and wildly manoeuvring ships, *Turbulent* was rammed and sunk by the battleship *Westfalen*. Ordinary Seaman Wood was among 87 men who lost their lives in the sinking. Only 13 men survived. George Obed Wood was aged 22 and is commemorated on the Naval Memorial at Chatham.

Assistant Steward Alec John Parkhurst, HMS *Hampshire*

Alec John Parkhurst was born at Westerham on 5 May 1887, the son of John and Louisa Parkhurst. His mother was for some time headmistress of the Gordon House School, Westerham. Alec John Parkhurst worked as a civil servant before enlisting in the Royal Navy at Portsmouth in March 1916. After training at the shore establishment HMS *Victory*, he joined the cruiser HMS *Hampshire* on 24 May working in the Paymasters department. *Hampshire*, of the 2nd Cruiser Squadron, served with the Grand Fleet based at Scapa Flow. Just six days after joining *Hampshire*, Parkhurst was in action at the Battle of Jutland, where his ship came through unscathed. However, after the return from Jutland, *Hampshire* was immediately detailed for a further mission. On 5 June, HMS *Hampshire* sailed from Scapa Flow carrying the Secretary of State for War, Lord Kitchener, on a military mission to Russia. Shortly after leaving harbour in atrocious weather, the ship struck a mine laid by a German U-boat. In all, 650 men, including Lord Kitchener and his staff, were lost. Alec John Parkhurst was among those who perished. He had been in the navy for three months and at sea for only two weeks. His name is commemorated on the Portsmouth naval memorial.

The news of Kitchener's death was met with shock and dismay throughout the country. The mortality of a man who appeared to embody the country's fighting spirit caused a sense of unease even among the ranks of the New Armies, who proudly referred to themselves as 'Kitchener's Men'. On Tuesday 13 June, simultaneously with a service at St Paul's Cathedral, a memorial service for Lord Kitchener was held at St Mary's church, Westerham. It was attended by the locally stationed troops and representatives of civic bodies as well as local citizens. The service was led by the Reverend Le Mesurier. (It is interesting to note this genuine and spontaneous mark of respect for a man who is now vilified by revisionist historians.)

In the summer of 1916 a steady stream of wounded soldiers were still arriving at the Dunsdale Hospital and Westerham people responded readily to appeals for food and comforts for the recovering and convalescent men. Items as diverse as pyjamas and pigeons, cigarettes and cucumbers were all donated in significant quantities. Convalescent soldiers were also entertained at tea parties at the larger houses of the district. As well as supplying socks and knitted garments for men at the Front and the local hospital, the National Service Committee also began collecting waste paper salvage as a further way of supporting the war effort.

As more men were drafted into the army, many local businesses began to suffer from manpower shortages. Many of the appeals against conscription heard at the Oxted and Sevenoaks tribunals were made by employers wishing to retain key staff. Hookers, the Westerham printers, appealed on behalf of two workers claiming they had already lost several staff members to the Colours and any further drain would be untenable for the business. A conditional exemption was granted for one man and a one month exemption for the other. Lord Weardale appealed on behalf of a Westerham electrician who maintained vital equipment on his estate, and a three-month exemption was granted to enable a replacement to be found. Another Westerham employer claimed that his business would have to close if his sons were made to join the army. This appeal was refused. At another tribunal Mr Bushell of the Westerham Brewery complained that he had earlier encouraged his staff to enlist with a £5 bounty, but was now down to his last engineer! A conditional exemption was granted. Also in the town, John Miles of Madan Road announced the closure of his cycle business as his call-up papers arrived.

Other departures from Westerham were the 2nd/1st Home Counties Brigade, Royal Field Artillery, leaving for France after many months billeted in the district. In the other direction, Sergeant Major Thomas Henry Martle, the Westerham Territorials instructor, came home to Stratton Terrace having been invalided from the Middle East. Elsewhere, the recently opened small bore rifle range in Squerryes Park was being put to good use by the Cadets and a local rifle club and during the school summer holidays older Hosey boys were organised to help at local farms with labour shortages. The Swan Cinema also kept up a good variety of films and for the energetic the Brasted swimming baths were still open. Empire Day was marked by flags flying on public buildings and at Hosey School the day was celebrated by the singing of patriotic songs.

* * *

Meanwhile, across the Channel in the summer of 1916, a new British Army was beginning to gather in a hitherto quiet corner of France. Men, horses, guns and equipment, on an unprecedented scale, were converging on an area of pleasant countryside that was previously untouched by war. Westerham men among the many thousands arriving would find the landscape strangely familiar. The intensely cultivated farmland with coppiced woods and small neat villages, set among gently rolling downland, was almost reminiscent of home. For the troops that had moved here from Flanders the change was positively refreshing. The broad roads and sparkling streams, together with towns that offered some measure of comfort and amenity, were all a welcome change from the ruin and desolation they had left behind in the north.

Yet the majority of the freshly arriving troops were not the veterans of the battles of 1914 and 1915. The newcomers were even more men of Kitchener's Army, straight from England, who after nearly two years of preparation and training were now deemed ready for battle. The coming offensive, to which these men would soon be committed, had been in plan since the previous winter. As all earlier attacks appeared to come unstuck through lack of shells and reinforcements, great hopes were placed on the projected battle. This time with enough guns, enough shells and above all enough men, surely the much sought-after breakthrough would be achieved. The coming battle would take its name from the dull, uninteresting river that meandered turgidly through the region in which the troops were gathering. Its name was the Somme.

For the men of the 1st Battalion, Royal West Kents, the move to the Somme in July 1916 ended a long period of relative calm and stability. Since the battles for Hill 60 in April and May of the previous year, the Battalion had taken part in no major action and, despite a drain of casualties through sickness and wounds, was now at full strength with just over 1,000 men. The ranks of the West Kents included several Westerham soldiers. Sidney Lambert, a former gamekeeper on the Squerryes estate, had joined the Battalion in May 1915. John Beard of Lodge

Lane and formerly of the Westerham brewery had also served in France for just over a year and William Arthur Weller, of the High Street and a former Cadet, had been with the Battalion since the beginning of 1916. Other Westerham men arriving on the Somme during that summer were Fred Yorkston from Madan Road with the 13th Rifle Brigade, Fred Gallup also of Madan Road with the 6th Royal West Kents and Henry Singleton from New Street serving with the Royal Field Artillery. Among the first to go into action were Sydney Charles King, also from New Street, of the Queen's Royal West Surreys and Archibald Ayres from the High Street, serving with the 7th Royal West Kents.

The Battle of the Somme began at 7.30 a.m. on 1 July 1916 when over 100,000 British infantrymen rose from their trenches in the initial assault. This first day of the Somme offensive would go down as one of the most disastrous in military history. Despite a preparatory artillery bombardment lasting six days, many of the assaulting troops advanced into uncut barbed wire and trenches manned by fully prepared defenders. By the end of the day the British casualties were nearly 20,000 dead with thousands more wounded. Of the Westerham men who went over the top on the first day, Archibald Ayres of the 7th Royal West Kents and Sydney Charles King of the 7th Queen's were both part of the attack on the fortified village of Montauban. Here, despite fierce opposition, the assault was largely successful with the attacking troops gaining nearly all their objectives. For Sydney King, however, the cost was a wound to the knee, due to which he was eventually invalided home.

Despite the losses of the first day, the Somme offensive ground on remorselessly through the month of July. As ever more men were drawn into the fighting, hospitals all over England stood by to receive the wounded from the front. William Martin from Railway Terrace, Westerham, serving with the Royal West Kents, was wounded in July and was evacuated to a hospital in Scotland. Other Westerham casualties of the early fighting were Henry Singleton of the Artillery – wounded in the arm; William Miles of the Royal Engineers from London Road – shell-shock;

and Fred Yorkston of the Rifle Brigade receiving a bullet through the shoulder in the fighting at Contalmaison.

By mid-July, the 1st Battalion, Royal West Kents began moving towards the Somme from the Arras sector by way of Herrisart, Franvillers and Meaulte. The Battalion reached the front line on 19th July and, on the 20th moved up to occupy the forward trenches between High Wood and the village of Longueval.

Private John Beard, 1st Battalion, Royal West Kent Regiment

John Beard was born at Limpsfield, Surrey, in 1877. He was the son of George and Eliza Beard and by 1901 the family was resident at 7 Lodge Lane, Westerham. John Beard attended Hosey School and was also a member of the local Volunteer Battalion. After leaving school he worked for many years as a drayman at the Westerham brewery. In February 1915 he enlisted in the Royal West Kent Regiment at Maidstone and after training he was posted to the 1st Battalion, landing in France on 1 May.

From May 1915 the 1st Royal West Kents took turns in the trenches, first at Ypres and later in the Somme region at Carnoy, in what was at that time a fairly quiet sector. Before returning to the Somme in July 1916 the Battalion had spent four months in the vicinity of Arras. On arrival in the Somme battle zone, the 1st Royal West Kents, as part of the 13th Infantry Brigade, were detailed to attack the German strongpoint of High Wood.

As the battalion moved up to the front line on the night of 19/20 July, the Germans put down a heavy bombardment, which caused severe casualties in one of the advancing companies. John Beard, who was among those wounded, died of his wounds the following day. He was later buried near the village of Montauban.

In the following years the tide of war twice more swept over the area and at the end of hostilities Beard's grave could not be identified. He is now listed among the missing of the battle and his name is commemorated on the Thiepval Memorial. This vast monument stands on the battlefield and carries the names of 73,000 men who died in the Somme battles with no known grave.

On the night of 22/23 July the 1st Royal West Kents assaulted the enemy trenches at High Wood in an action that gained some lodgements in the German lines but at a terrible cost in casualties. Eventually, not even these lodgements could be maintained and the survivors were withdrawn to their original positions.

Much of the fighting in July and August centred on control of the coppiced woods that were scattered among the open Somme countryside. In a largely featureless landscape, the woods of Trones, Delville, Bernafray and High Wood provided natural defensive strongpoints, which the Germans put to good use. After an attack on Trones Wood in mid-July, two companies of the 7th Royal West Kents found themselves cut off and surrounded. In a stand that was widely acclaimed, the Royal West Kents fought off repeated counter-attacks before being relieved. Archibald Ayres of High Street, Westerham, was among those who came safely through the action.

The Battle of the Somme raged on through the month of July and into August. The fighting inevitably sucked in more units, many with Westerham men serving. In early August, the British had still not wrested High Wood from German control and fierce fighting continued around the village of Longueval and the adjacent Delville Wood. During the artillery duels that thundered across the front line in August 1916, Westerham would suffer a further casualty to the Somme fighting.

Gunner George Alfred Douglas Shearing, 167th Brigade, Royal Field Artillery

George Alfred Douglas Shearing was born in 1890, the son of George and Emma Shearing of 9 South Bank,

Westerham. He was a former Hosey boy and member of the town band. He worked for Durtnells the builders prior to enlisting in the Artillery as a volunteer at the beginning of the war, and served in France from December 1915. During the summer of 1916 the 167th Brigade, Royal Field Artillery moved to the Somme and by August were in almost continual action on the sector between High Wood and the village of Longueval. Gunner Shearing was killed in action on 14 August in the shell-swept area to the south of High Wood known to the troops as 'Caterpillar Valley'. He is buried in the nearby Quarry Cemetery just north of the village of Montauban. This cemetery, which takes its name from the adjacent quarry that once gave sanctuary to the wounded, contains the graves of many artillerymen who died in the fighting of August 1916.

Private Charles James Fisk, 10th Battalion, Australian Infantry

The Australians who had fought at Gallipoli were withdrawn to Egypt when the peninsula was evacuated at the end of 1915. After some months of rest and training they made their way via the south of France towards the Somme, arriving in mid-July 1916.

Many of the Australians who had spent months on the Gallipoli peninsula were now veteran fighters. For Charles James Fisk, formerly of Westerham and serving in the 10th Australian Infantry, it was almost a year since he was first in action. Having left Westerham some five years earlier, he had first resided in the Coorabie district of South Australia. He enlisted in the Australian forces at the outbreak of war and landed at Gallipoli in August 1915, in time for the Battle of Lone Pine and the desperate attempt to break out of the beachhead.

After Gallipoli, Fisk spent some weeks in hospital in Egypt, where he was surprised to receive one of the Christmas parcels donated by the Westerham townspeople. In a letter to Reverend Le Mesurier, published in the *Westerham Herald*, he expressed his gratitude and surprise at being remembered after so long away from the town.

After six months away from the war, the Australians went into action on the Somme against the fortified village of Pozieres on 23 July 1916. For the following weeks the Australians were engaged in the fierce, yard-by-yard fighting that typified the Somme battle. The 10th Australians were to gain a VC for their action at Pozieres. By August the Australians were attacking Mouquet Farm (inevitably 'Mucky Farm' to the troops) which, in reality, was another strongly fortified German position.

Charles Fisk was killed in action during this period of intense fighting on 23 August 1916. The sad news was conveyed to his parents at Westerham. Private Fisk was 28, and among the many who were never found after the battle. His name is commemorated on the memorial at Villers Brettoneux, France, which records the Australian 'missing' of the First World War.

The Somme fighting raged through August and into September with the Germans contesting and counter-attacking for every yard of ground gained. The battle swung to and fro at Delville Wood while High Wood, despite all the effort, was still in enemy hands. In a massive attack that was planned for 15 September, the British would assault six miles of German front between the villages of Courcelette and Ginchy. This time a new secret weapon would be employed. A number of tracked armoured vehicles recently brought over from England would advance with the infantry with the object of overrunning enemy strongpoints. These vehicles were code named 'tanks'.

Private Richard Heathcote Blackaby, 1st Battalion, East Kent Regiment

Richard Heathcote Blackaby was born in Gloucestershire, the son of the Reverend and Mrs F.E. Blackaby of the Manse, Eastcombe, near Stroud. Richard was an employee of the Westminster and County Bank and worked at the branch in Westerham's market square from April 1913. While at Westerham, he was an active member of the Congregational church.

He volunteered for the army in February 1915, joining the Buffs (East Kent Regiment), and served in France with the 1st Battalion, which arrived on the Somme in August 1916. In the attack of 15 September, the 1st Buffs were detailed to assault a German strongpoint known as the Quadrilateral Redoubt, situated near the village of Ginchy. The position consisted of a warren of earthworks and dugouts protected by nests of machine guns and barbed wire. The attack by the Buffs would be supported by tanks on their first ever day in action. At 6.20 a.m. on 15 September the Buffs and the 8th Bedfords (in which another Westerham man, Sergeant H.V. Hobbis, was serving), advanced over open ground towards their objectives. Sadly, the tanks supporting the Buffs attack were all ditched or disabled, leaving the troops exposed to withering machine-gun fire. In a largely unsuccessful action, the 1st Buffs suffered grievous losses, Private Blackaby being among those wounded. He succumbed to his wounds three days later and was buried near the village of Meaulte. A commemorative plaque bearing the name of R.H. Blackaby still stands, largely unnoticed, on a wall within the present Natwest Bank, Westerham.

In the attack of 15 September, other tanks successfully cleared German trenches near the northern tip of Delville Wood, ending weeks of desperate fighting in the wood's vicinity. The 8th Battalion, Royal West Kents, was one of many units to have fought in the earlier battles for Delville Wood and by mid-September they were withdrawn to a quiet sector to rest and refit. In October, the Battalion was again taking turns in the trenches, this time in the mining area of northern France near to the scene of the 1915 Battle of Loos. In the ranks of B Company since the battalion's arrival in France, just over one year earlier, was a 28-year-old Westerham man, George Harry Fennell.

Corporal George Harry Fennell, 8th Battalion, Royal West Kent Regiment

George Harry Fennell was born in 1888, the son of Albert and Elizabeth Fennell of Force Green, Westerham. He attended Hosey School before working as a cowman at Force Green Farm. He was married in 1914 and later worked at a farm near Haywards Heath, Sussex. He enlisted in the army on 6 January 1915, joining the 8th Royal West Kents, which was then forming at Shoreham, Sussex. He was described on attestation as a 'smart and intelligent recruit'. The 8th Royal West Kents landed in France in August 1915 and on their first ever day in action they were committed to an attack on 26 September, the second day of the Battle of Loos. In this disastrous action the Battalion suffered over 500 casualties. George Fennell was one of the few to come through unscathed.

The 8th Royal West Kents fought on the Somme from August 1916 and after again taking heavy casualties were withdrawn, via Abbeville, to a relatively quiet sector near Bethune. From October 1916 the Battalion took turns in the trenches at Hulluch and was engaged in general trench warfare.

On the night of 21 November, Corporal Fennell was part of a patrol about to enter no man's-land when he was struck by a mortar bomb and killed instantly. He was buried just behind the lines at the Philosophie British cemetery, Marzingarbe, France. His wife, Alice Fennell, who later lived at Manor Cottages, Westerham, was awarded a pension of 15 shillings a week.

Corporal Arthur Clemans, 91st Siege Battery, Royal Garrison Artillery

While the 8th West Kents were away from the Somme fighting, the battle had continued as fiercely as ever. In November 1916 the British were again contesting the villages to the north of the Somme, which had been the objectives back in July.

On 17 November, Arthur Clemans of the 91st Siege Battery, Royal Garrison Artillery, stationed near the village of Mailly Maillet, had been in action continuously for three days. The RGA gunners manned the army's heavy guns and howitzers, and were pounding the German lines near Beaumont Hamel.

Clemans, whose family lived at Court Lodge Farm, Westerham, had been in the army for over seven years. Prior to enlisting he had been a Hosey boy and had also worked as a clerk for the Southern Railway Company. After joining the army, he had spent nearly five years in India. Now, on 17 November, the gunners laboured at their guns, firing at a rate of one round per gun per minute. At 4 p.m. that afternoon the breechblock of the gun Arthur Clemans was serving blew out, killing him and two other gunners. He is buried in Mailly Wood cemetery, Somme, France.

The Battle of the Somme is officially considered to have lasted from 1 July to 18 November 1916. In nearly five months of fighting the army had sustained something in the order of 350,000 casualties – killed, wounded or missing. In terms of territory gained, the maximum advance was no more than six miles, less than was hoped for on the first day. In later years, attempts were made to justify the battle in terms of wearing down the enemy. Even today it is difficult to assess which side suffered the most in what became largely a battle of attrition.

For many communities the cost had been appalling. In the North of England, where individual towns had raised their own battalions, the men who had enlisted together and gone into battle together had consequently died together. Five Westerham men had died in the fighting and at least a further ten had been seriously wounded. Fred Gallop, from Madan Road, with the 6th Royal West Kents, was twice wounded, first in July and again in the September, to a severity from which he was discharged the following year. Henry Russell Hoath of South Bank, serving with the London Regiment, was wounded on 1 October. He was later invalided home. William Hayward, the former Westerham postman in the Royal Sussex, was wounded for the second time and found himself recovering at the Dunsdale Hospital. The anxiety of families with menfolk at the front can scarcely be imagined.

For John Bateman of Horns Hill, Westerham, the recent months had been particularly stressful. In August his son-in-law Sidney Lambert had been reported wounded and in hospital at Boulogne. His daughter Nellie had been permitted to cross the Channel to visit her husband at the hospital – always a sign that the wounds were extremely serious. Then, in November, the news had arrived that his own son John of the Royal Susssex Regiment had sustained wounds to his neck, side and left arm. For families throughout the town the arrival of a War Office telegram bringing news of a son or husband, wounded or perhaps worse, was anticipated with dread.

The frailty of human life at that time was further demonstrated by the death of a Westerham soldier, Richard Wallace Wade, who, despite being a family man of some years, had felt it his duty to enlist. His death through natural causes was no less a tragedy for his family.

Private Richard Wallace Wade, 3rd Battalion, Royal Sussex Regiment

Richard Wallace Wade of Brewery Cottages, Westerham, caused some surprise when, at the age of 42, he volunteered for the army. Given that he suffered from generally poor health, it was a further surprise when he was accepted into the Royal Sussex Regiment. Wade worked at the Westerham brewery near his home and was a married man with a son and two daughters. After enlisting, he was stationed with his regiment at Newhaven, Sussex.

In November 1916 he was admitted to hospital at Newhaven where he died on the 28th. On Monday 3 December, his funeral took place at Westerham. A cortège led by troops from the locally stationed Herts Yeomanry left the family home in the High Street for the parish church. After a service conducted by the Reverend Le Mesurier, Private Wade was buried in St Mary's churchyard while volleys were fired over the grave and trumpeters sounded the Last Post.

Although the fighting on the Somme abated with the onset of winter, the sector was still very active with considerable local fighting for positions that gave small tactical advantage. Troops in the front line endured worsening conditions as the weather deteriorated and the ground dissolved into seas of mud. Reliefs and supplies often had to be brought across miles of shell-torn countryside ensuring that men were exhausted on reaching the front line and rations were stone cold by the time they were distributed. Once there, the troops suffered intense cold and discomfort while often standing knee-deep in mud and slime. At all times there was constant danger from snipers, mortar fire and enemy counter-attacks. The Somme battlefield would claim the life of a further Westerham man before the close of 1916.

2nd Lieutenant Arthur Baldry, 14th Battalion, York and Lancaster Regiment

Arthur Baldry was born in the Lake District on 11 July 1887, the son of Arthur and Jane Baldry of 'Cooks House', Windermere. He grew up in the Lake District and after attending university came to Westerham in 1909 to work on the staff of the Pilgrim House School. During his time at Westerham, he became a trainee for the priesthood and was later ordained. Baldry preached at St Mary's church on many occasions. Shortly after the outbreak of war he volunteered for military service, joining the Royal Army Medical Corps on 2 November 1914.

In 1916, Baldry gained a commission and was subsequently appointed to the 14th Battalion of the York and Lancaster Regiment. He joined his battalion on 29 August 1916 at Neuve Chapelle, France. The 14th Yorks and Lancs was a Kitchener battalion raised almost exclusively in the South Yorkshire town of Barnsley, and their unofficial title was the 2nd Barnsley Pals. The Battalion had landed in France in 1916 having first been sent to Egypt. The 14th Yorks and Lancs had gone into action on the first day of the Somme against the village of Serre where they suffered heavy losses. After the attack, they were withdrawn to a quiet sector but had returned to the battle in October.

In November, the Battalion again took turns in the trenches at Serre, near to the area they attacked so disastrously on 1 July. On being relieved, the Battalion moved to Sailly au Bois on 22 November. At the beginning of December they once more moved back to the front line where, on the 4th, they came under heavy shellfire. One report of that day states that a young soldier became unhinged in the bombardment and ran out into no man's land. In an attempted rescue, Baldry rushed after the soldier and in so doing was shot by an enemy sniper. The war diary of the 14th Yorks and Lancs for 4 December

61

1916 simply states: 'Enemy shelled our trenches in left sector. Much aerial activity on both sides. Weather very clear and fine. 2nd Lt. A Baldry killed in action.'

Arthur Baldry died aged 29 and is buried at the nearby Sailly au Bois military cemetery.

The losses of battalions like the 14th Yorks and Lancs in the Somme fighting caused a radical rethink in the British command on how infantry units should be manned. It had become painfully clear that when a battalion raised in a specific locality went into battle, particularly costly actions like the Somme, then the casualties would fall disproportionally on that community. The town of Barnsley had suffered over 200 men killed on just the first day of the attack. In towns like Leeds, Sheffield and Belfast the figures were even higher. Although the advantages of local enthusiasm and identity were welcomed at the outset, it was obvious that a change in policy was necessary to prevent a catastrophe befalling the menfolk of closely identified communities, and the communities themselves.

This new policy would also have implications for Westerham soldiers who had previously naturally gravitated to the Royal West Kent Regiment. Although no Royal West Kent battalion had been raised on an individual locality (apart from the 11th, raised in the London borough of Lewisham), men who enlisted after 1916 found themselves allocated to regiments on a purely 'as needed' basis. This policy applied not only to new recruits but also to returning wounded and even to men returning from leave. Soldiers arriving at base depots in France often found themselves summarily packaged off to unfamiliar units in a totally random fashion. This was naturally a source of great resentment, with men drafted away from comrades and familiar surroundings, even more so among old soldiers, brought up in the regimental tradition, who always saw themselves as a 'Fusilier', a 'West Kent' or a 'Queen's Soldier'. The policy did not even end at one regimental move. In the course of the war, some men served in three or more regiments.

The record for a Westerham soldier appears to be William

Stephen Sales of Palin's Cottages, Vicarage Hill, who, in a distinguished war service, was wounded, received a Divisional Recommendation and served in the Royal West Kents, the Middlesex, the Royal Fusiliers and the London Regiment.

* * *

As 1916 drew to a close, Westerham prepared for another wartime Christmas. Once again gifts and parcels were handed in at the vicarage for onward dispatch to local men at the Front. The National Service Committee workroom appealed for more knitters so that extra gloves, mittens and socks could be sent to the men in the trenches. Another 118 articles were completed in time for Christmas.

St Mary's Hall was again busy as a troop canteen, this time for the Hertfordshire Yeomanry who had arrived to be billeted in the town in November. Concerts and dances were arranged at the Hall for the holiday period and once again the Men's Club threw its doors open to the visiting soldiers.

An appeal was also made for gifts and comforts for the wounded at the Dunsdale Hospital. Mr Boddy's butcher shop ran a 'guess the weight of the turkey' competition at 6d a ticket, the proceeds being donated to the hospital. On Christmas Day, each wounded soldier awoke to find a filled Christmas stocking and later a dinner of turkey and ham was served. A small concert followed in the afternoon. At St Mary's church, the services over Christmas and the New Year ended before dark to conserve power and to assist with the blackout regulations then in force against prowling Zeppelins.

1917

After nearly two and a half years of fighting, 1917 began in much the same way as the beginnings of 1915 and 1916. The opposing armies on the Western Front still faced each other across a frozen wasteland of mud and desolation with little to show for all the effort and sacrifice of the previous year. In some cases the limited territorial gains of recent offensives had left the attackers in a more precarious tactical position than before the attack. In the shell-torn moonscape of the old Somme battlefield men suffered frostbite and exposure in the frozen, waterlogged trenches. The deadlocked trench warfare seemed as intractable as ever.

At Christmas 1916, the 1st Royal West Kents had been out of the line and in billets near Bethune, France. The first weeks of 1917 were spent in intensive training but there was still time for occasional band concerts, cinema shows and sports competitions. The Battalion returned to the line on 14 January. The New Year found the 6th West Kents near Arras and the 7th Battalion resting and refitting near Abbeville. The 8th Battalion spent the winter taking turns in the trenches close to the old Loos battlefield. Despite this apparent inactivity, all units in the front line suffered continual losses due to sporadic shelling, sniping and trench raids.

The French and British commanders who met that winter to consider the options for the year ahead could only agree on one plan – to return to the offensive in the coming spring. To this end, it was planned that the French Army would launch a large-scale attack in the Champagne region to the south while the British, as a diversion to the main French attack, would assault the Germans on the Arras front. Before then, however, the continuing trench warfare in the winter of 1917 would cause more heartbreak for Westerham families.

Corporal William Arthur Weller, 1st Battalion, Royal West Kent Regiment

William Arthur Weller was born at Westerham in 1889, the son of Thomas and Sarah Weller of 'New Rose Villa'. The Wellers were well known building contractors in Westerham with premises just off the High Street. William Arthur Weller attended Hosey School and was a prominent member of the Cadet Corps where he rose to the rank of Colour Sergeant. He served with the Territorials from the outbreak of war before transferring to the 1st Battalion, Royal West Kents. He was married shortly before leaving for France in January 1916. Weller served with the 1st Royal West Kents on the Somme in the summer of 1916.

At the beginning of 1917 the 1st West Kents were near Festubert in a relatively quiet sector. However, on 10 February, the Battalion was detailed to carry out a large-scale raid on the German trenches at Givenchy. The raid was to be carried out in daylight and at battalion strength. Under cover of an intense bombardment, the West Kents left their trenches and, crossing no man's land, penetrated the enemy defences, bombing dugouts and capturing over 30 prisoners. The raiders returned to their trenches after 40 minutes but suffered casualties from a counter-bombardment. The raid, which was considered an outstanding success by the command, cost the Battalion 16 killed and 54 wounded. Corporal Weller was among those who lost their lives, he was aged 29 and is buried nearby at Gorre British Cemetery, France.

Private William Jesse Bird, 7th Battalion, Royal West Kent Regiment

William Jesse Bird was born at Westerham in 1889, the son of Thomas and Annie Bird of Lodge Lane. He attended

Hosey School and in August 1914 was serving with the West Kent Yeomanry, a cavalry unit of the Territorial Army. Whilst at Maidstone, he transferred into the Royal West Kents and was later posted to the 7th Battalion in France. The 7th Royal West Kents fought on the Somme during the summer of 1916 and in November was withdrawn from the fighting and spent two months of respite in the Abbeville area. Here it carried out training, sports, and absorbed drafts from the regimental depot to make good its losses.

In mid-February 1917, the 7th West Kents returned to the line in the vicinity of Grandcourt on the Somme battlefield. Here they were immediately ordered to carry out an attack to regain a trench that was partially in German control. The attack was launched in the early hours of 14 February 1917. The operation was to end in confusion with part of the attacking force losing direction and being stopped by uncut barbed wire. The objectives of the attack were only partially gained and at great cost in casualties. The futility of this purely 'tidying up' enterprise was emphasised when the Germans began withdrawing from the area to newly-prepared defensive positions just three days later. John Beard, aged 28, was killed in this attack and has no known grave. He is listed on the Thiepval Memorial.

In Westerham the year of 1917 had begun in sombre mood. Many men were now at home recovering from wounds from the previous year and even more were leaving the town to serve in the army. Mrs Douglas, of Farley House, whose own sons were serving in France, began compiling a roll of honour, which named the men of the parish then serving in uniform. By the time the roll was displayed in St Mary's Hall the list exceeded 300 names. Many of these men already serving at the front wrote to acknowledge the Christmas parcels collected and distributed by the Reverend Le Mesurier. A selection of thank-you letters was printed in the *Westerham Herald.*

The gravity of the war situation was also manifesting itself in an increasing scarcity of food and other commodities. A series of lectures was given by Walter Rowe, the head gardener of Squerryes, in which he stressed the importance of 'war crops' and also gave advice on the efficient use of gardens and allotments. The meetings, at which Dr Russell presided, were held at St Mary's Hall. In a small relief from the prevailing mood, the severe weather that ushered in the New Year enabled skating to take place on the Long Pond opposite the brewery.

Elsewhere, January 1917 had seen a bizarre Westerham reunion in mercifully warmer surroundings. On 11 January, George Thomas Gardiner of Westerham was on board the destroyer HMS *Beagle* as she approached Malta, escorting the battleship *Cornwallis*. Unbeknown to the British squadron, the *Cornwallis* was being stalked by a German submarine. Just a few miles from Malta two torpedoes struck the *Cornwallis* which began to sink. After carrying out random depth charging, the *Beagle* drew alongside the stricken battleship to take off survivors. Among those rescued, George Gardiner was able to welcome two Westerham sailors, William Bashford of Park Cottages, and John Baker.

* * *

The German withdrawal from the Somme battlefield which began in February 1917 was initially viewed as an encouraging development. The retreating Germans were pursued cautiously at first but it soon became apparent that their army was disengaging on a front that extended some 40 miles from Arras to the River Aisne. The French and British armies, following through a landscape devastated by the retreating Germans, soon found themselves confronted by an even more elaborate system of defences which had been constructed during the previous winter. This new defensive position, known as the Hindenburg Line, enabled the Germans to shorten their front with a consequent saving of manpower, while for the attacking Allies it meant starting all over again. Yet, as the proposed British and

French spring offensive lay at the extremities of the German withdrawal, it was decided that the attack could go ahead as previously planned. Consequently, on Easter Monday, 9 April 1917 at 5.30 a.m., the British 3rd Army launched the Battle of Arras while at the same time the Canadian Corps assaulted and captured Vimy Ridge.

The attack was initially successful. Thanks to good artillery preparation, the attacking troops were able to advance in places by up to three miles. However, in the days that followed, the impetus of the attack faltered while the German defences stiffened and casualties began to mount. In the south, the French attack had gone disastrously wrong with losses from which the French Army never fully recovered. The failure of the French offensive in the Champagne region condemned the British to continue the pressure on the Arras front. This was to have terrible consequences for Westerham families.

Private Charles Terry, 17th Battalion, Middlesex Regiment

Charles Terry, a married man who lived at Hosey Hill, enlisted in the Royal West Kent Regiment at Westerham. He was born at Limpsfield, Surrey, in 1875 and had later moved to Westerham and attended Hosey School. In 1901 his family is listed as living at Copthall Cottage on Vicarage Hill. He served in France from 1916, initially with the Royal West Kents but subsequently with the 17th Battalion Middlesex Regiment, soon to be committed to the Battle of Arras.

By the middle of April 1917 the British 3rd Army at Arras had gained most of the objectives of the initial attack and was also engaging the German reserves in the area. However, in order to support the struggling French offensive and prevent the transfer of German troops to the south, the attack was ordered to continue. As part of the renewed offensive, the 17th Middlesex attacked at

Oppy Wood to the east of Arras, going over the top at 4.30 a.m. on 28 April. The attacking troops entered the German first line but were later driven out by a counter-attack after heavy fighting. On the following day only 42 men of the Middlesex answered the roll call. Private Terry was among those listed as missing and his family never received any further news of his fate. Charles Terry is named on the Arras Memorial, France.

Private Norrie Alfred Leney, 22nd Battalion, Royal Fusiliers

Norrie Alfred Leney was born at Westerham in 1876, the son of Alfred and Kitty Leney of New Street. He was a former Hosey boy and prior to enlisting, his occupation was a butcher. He enlisted in the Royal West Kents at Maidstone and served in France from 1916.

In 1917 he was among the many soldiers who were required to change regiments as the service demanded. By the time of the Battle of Arras in April 1917 he was serving in the 22nd Battalion, Royal Fusiliers. This battalion was committed to the same attack just one day after the action in which Charles Terry was killed.

At 4 a.m. on 29 April, the 22nd Royal Fusiliers advanced against the defences of Oppy Wood but were barred by impenetrable belts of barbed wire, the Battalion suffering grievous casualties as a result. Private Leney, aged 41, was among those missing after the attack. His body was never recovered and he is also listed on the Arras Memorial, which commemorates 35,000 men who died fighting in the vicinity of Arras and who have no known grave.

Sergeant Tom Quaife, 6th Battalion, East Kent Regiment

On the 19 May 1917, the news reached Westerham of a further local casualty in the savage fighting at Arras. The family of former Hosey boy Thomas Quaife received a letter from a comrade confirming that Tom had been killed by shellfire while resting out of the line. Tom, a former Cadet, had worked for the builders Durtnells of Brasted prior to enlisting. He had served in France with the 6th Battalion, East Kent Regiment.

In April 1917, the Battalion took part in the opening attack at Arras and was later involved in bitter fighting near the village of Monchy-le-Preux. The Battalion was again in the vicinity of Monchy on 1 May when Tom was killed. The letter sent to his mother also stated that Tom had come safely through an earlier attack. Tom Quaife was aged 19 when he died.

Three Westerham men – Charles Terry, Norrie Alfred Leney and Thomas Quaife – had all died in the same battle within the space of four days. It stands as a testament to the savage and brutal nature of the fighting at Arras that none of these men were ever found. All three are now commemorated on the Arras Memorial.

Private Edward Charles Smith, 7th Battalion, Royal West Kent Regiment

The fighting at Arras that continued into the month of May was to cost the life of a further Westerham soldier. Edward Charles Smith, born at Kent Hatch and a former Hosey boy, had enlisted in the Royal West Kents at Tonbridge. He was a married man who lived in Lodge Lane and had earlier worked at the Westerham brewery. He served with the 7th Battalion, which fought almost continuously at Arras from the first day, 9 April 1917.

Towards the end of May the 7th West Kents were in the front line east of Arras near the village of Fontaine-le-Croiselles. Private Smith was killed in action on 27 May. He is buried at the nearby British cemetery at Heninel, France.

* * *

Although the Western Front in France and Flanders was always the crucial area of fighting, the war also continued in a number of other more distant theatres. Despite the Gallipoli campaign having ended in early 1916, the Turks were still being engaged in the Middle East on a number of fronts. In Mesopotamia (now Iraq), a British army was advancing cautiously along the rivers Tigris and Euphrates towards Baghdad. In Egypt the Turks had briefly threatened the Suez Canal during 1915 and even by 1916 there was only an uneasy no man's land between the two armies across the Sinai peninsula. Many of the troops fighting in the Middle East belonged to the Territorial units originally sent overseas to release the regular army for fighting in France. Among the Territorials enduring the harsh and arid conditions of the Sinai Desert was the 2nd/4th Battalion of the Royal West Kent Regiment. The Royal West Kents had originally proceeded overseas to Gallipoli but had been withdrawn to Egypt after the evacuation. In early 1917 they had taken part in the Battle of Gaza where the fighting had bogged down in the all too familiar stalemate of trench warfare. Among the West Kents were several Westerham men including George William Barnett of Palin's Cottages, Vicarage Hill.

Private George William Barnett, 2nd/4th Battalion, Royal West Kent Regiment

George William Barnett was born in 1893, the son of George and Sarah Barnett of High Street, Westerham. He attended Hosey School and was also a volunteer in the Territorial Army. By the outbreak of war in 1914 his family was living at Palin's Cottages, Vicarage Hill. He enlisted in the Royal West Kents at Tonbridge and served overseas with the 2nd/4th Battalion, which was stationed in Egypt from 1916. After the Battle of Gaza in April 1917, the West Kents remained in the vicinity, training and taking turns in the front line. While in a reserve area, the Battalion suffered an air attack, which caused over 70 casualties. Private Barnett was among those wounded and he later succumbed to his wounds. A married man, he died on 28 May 1917 and was buried in Port Said War Memorial cemetery. His brother Peter also served in the Royal West Kents in the Great War.

Rifleman Albert Bone, 2nd/12th Battalion, London Regiment

Although the intensity of fighting on the Arras front abated after May 1917, it was still far from being a quiet sector. Local fighting continued and even during so-called 'quiet periods' there was a steady flow of casualties from sniping, periodic shelling and occasional local attacks. In July 1917, Albert Bone from Hill Park, Westerham, was serving with the 2nd/12th Battalion of the London Regiment. The 2nd/12th Londons, a Territorial unit, was at that time in the vicinity of Bertincourt, south of Arras. On the night of 8 July, the Battalion entered the trenches at Havrincourt Wood, relieving the 1st/5th Manchesters. For the next few days the Londons observed trench routine, enduring some artillery and mortar bombardments and also conducted active patrolling in the hours of darkness. On the night of 12 July, the Londons sent out a fighting patrol some 20 strong to reconnoitre a local strong point. This patrol was detected and came under heavy fire. Six men, including Albert Bone, were wounded. Albert died of wounds the following day. Albert Bone, age 38, who was the son of John and Agnes Bone is buried at the British cemetery, Manancourt, France.

Westerham had paid a heavy price in the recent fighting. Besides those killed and missing, a steady flow of wounded had also come home from the Front. Alfred (Jimmy) Allen, with the Royal West Kents, had been buried several times as a result of shellfire. He was invalided suffering from shell-shock and subsequently discharged. John Terry of Church Alley was wounded on 28 April in the same action from which his brother Charles was still missing. Albert Wood of Forge Cottage received two bullet wounds on 19 April and William Keeley of Madan Road, serving with the Royal Fusiliers, was invalided with gas poisoning. Two brothers from French Street were also wounded – Horace Wood of the Royal West Kents with a gunshot wound to the arm and Albert Henry Wood of the Queen's Westminster Rifles with wounds to the shoulder.

* * *

With the war now well into its third year, shortages of many commodities, notably foodstuffs, were all too apparent. Many farms were stripped of workers and even before the submarine crisis reached its peak, there was only a limited amount of shipping available to import food. A nationwide 'Food Economy Campaign' was instituted in May 1917 and a local committee was established for Westerham and district.

The Food Campaign held a number of public meetings in St Mary's Hall at which guest speakers urged the strictest economy with food. The speakers encouraged the use of 'Kilner' jars to preserve vegetables as well as fruit, and fruit-drying was also suggested as an alternative to jam-making as a measure towards conserving sugar. The optimum use of gardens and allotments for crop-growing was also emphasised. The Westerham Gardeners' Society had already decided to suspend its summer meetings as it was felt that the members' time would be better spent on their own gardens and allotments.

Elsewhere, the Reverend Le Mesurier announced that due to a shortage of labour only a limited care of the churchyard could be undertaken while the Swan Cinema closed its doors for the duration, the staff being diverted to war work. The Hertfordshire

Yeomanry left the town in July after many months billeted in the district. On a happier note, Miss Bartlett of Farley Croft presented 'Good Attendance' medals at Hosey School. W. Fuller, S. Vaus and W. Taylor all received awards for five years' perfect attendance. The ceremony concluded with a rendering of the national anthem accompanied by John Hooker on the violin.

In June the *Westerham Herald* reported that John Warde of Squerryes Court had passed out of the Military Academy at Woolwich and received a commission in the Royal Artillery. In August the *Herald* also announced the death of one of Westerham's long-standing citizens, Harry Martin of Madan Road.

Sergeant Harry Martin, 3rd/4th Battalion, Royal West Kent Regiment

Harry Martin of 'The Larches', Madan Road, was something of a local character. A bricklayer by trade, he was born at Headcorn, Kent, in 1865 but for as long as anyone could remember he had been associated with the local Volunteer Company of the Royal West Kents. For over 30 years he served with the Volunteers and the Territorials, latterly as a sergeant with the 3rd/4th Royal West Kents stationed at Canterbury. His only son Horace was also in the West Kents and had recently been posted to France. At over 50 years of age, he was clearly too old for active service and he also suffered from health problems. In 1916 he was discharged from the Army on medical grounds and subsequently came home to Westerham.

Harry Martin died at home on 28 August 1917. On Saturday, 1 September he was given a full military funeral at St Mary's Church. After the service, Sergeant Martin was buried in the churchyard as volleys were fired over the grave and Westerham's bandmaster Albert Newton sounded the Last Post.

Perhaps the most significant new dimension of warfare introduced during the First World War was that of air fighting. The first powered flight had only taken place some ten years earlier so that, by the outbreak of war, such aircraft as were available to the forces were often regarded as having little more than novelty value. The small air group that had landed in France with the British Expeditionary Force in 1914 had been used for reconnaissance and scouting, and had not always been taken seriously by the high command. All this was to change very rapidly as the true potential of the aeroplane became apparent. By 1917, air combat, artillery spotting and long-range aerial bombing, carried out by faster and more powerful aircraft, had become important aspects of the war.

The proximity of German air bases just across the Channel in Belgium meant that much of southern England was well within range of enemy air attack. Initially, these attacks had been carried out by Zeppelin airships. The first raid of the war took place as early as January 1915 when Zeppelins crossed East Anglia, bombing towns between Great Yarmouth and King's Lynn. As the war progressed, the raids increased in frequency and intensity. Although never reaching the scale of the Second World War Blitz, the raids were far more serious than mere nuisance value. In the summer and autumn of 1917 airship and aircraft raids on London and the south coast took place almost nightly, causing hundreds of casualties and widespread damage. On the night of 3/4 September 1917, there occurred one of the worst air raid incidents of the entire war. German Gotha twin-engined bombers took off from bases in Belgium to bomb targets in Kent between Margate and the Medway towns. A total of 46 bombs were dropped, two of which landed on the naval barracks at Chatham with terrible consequences.

'Uncle Charlie'
Serjeant Charles Albert Bateman, Royal West Kent Regiment.

Westerham around the turn of the century. The Wolfe Statue has yet to be erected.

The Green, Westerham.

High Street, Westerham, looking east.

Long pond, Westerham, looking towards Verrall's Corner. The brewery is the large building on the left.

The Cadet H.Q. at Verrall's Corner.

The Wolfe Statue is unveiled by Lord Roberts, 2nd January 1911.

The Cadets and Territorials at the unveiling of the Wolfe Statue.

Westerham Cadets at camp in 1913.

Westerham Cadets at camp with the 3rd Londons.

The Cadets at camp.
H. Howard meets a Fusilier
of the 3rd Londons.

Westerham Territorials arriving at summer camp, July 1914. War was declared one week later. Charles Bateman is nearest the camera.

3rd/4th Royal West Kents.

West Kent Territorials in loose order. George William Barnet is to the rear of the nearest rank, the first of two men with sloped rifles.

The 2nd West Lancashire Brigade Royal Field Artillery arrive at Westerham, October 1914.

The 2nd West Lancs RFA at Westerham

Church parade 1915.

The 2nd West Lancs RFA at Westerham

Local boys meet the Gunners.

The Gunners parade in front of the Crown Hotel.

Mr and Mrs Tattersall of London Road, Westerham. *Left to right back row:* Corporal Hobson, Gunner Hall, Trumpeter Jackson, Driver Jackson, Driver Beesdale, *Front Row:* Trumpeter Whipp, Trumpeter Lindsey, Trumpeter Stockdale.

The 'West Lancs' harness cleaning.

A muddy detail at Madan Road, Oak Lodge is in the background.

The West Lancs Field Ambulance at Westerham. View towards the North Downs.

Dunsdale House, Westerham, used as a Red Cross Hospital, 1914.

The wounded at the Dunsdale Hospital. Dr. Russell and Miss Watney are seated centre.

2nd Lieutenant A.H. Lang
Grenadier Guards
Killed in action on 25th January 1915.

Captain Allen Grant Douglas
London Scottish
Awarded the Military Cross
Killed in action on 30th November 1917.

Lt. Col. Percy William Beresford, D.S.O.
Westerham's Curate and founder of the
Cadets.
Died of wounds 26th October 1917.

Lieutenant John Alfred Pigou Inglis
Royal Engineers
Killed in action at the Battle of Loos,
25th September 1915.

Rev. Arthur Baldry
2nd Lieut. York and Lancaster Regt.
Killed in action on 4th December 1916.

Captain Ian Campbell Penney
13th Royal Scots
Killed in action at the Battle of Loos,
26th September 1915.

Flight Sub-Lieutenenant H G Brackley
Awarded the D.S.O. and D.S.C.
A former Hosey pupil from High Street.

Rev. Sydney Le Mesurier
Vicar of Westerham, 1900-1920.

William Stanley Gooding of South Bank
Killed by shellfire on 31st May 1918.

George Walter Allen of Mill Street
Killed in action aged 18 on 26th October
1917.

Sydney Charles King of New Street
Died of wounds in Italy on 7th January
1918.

Robert English of Mill Street
Died in Belgium on 8th February 1919.

Richard Charles Shergold of 'Rook's Nest'
Wounded in 1917.

Fred Shergold of 'Rook's Nest'
Royal Army Medical Corps.

Arthur Frederick Finch of New Street
Royal Garrison Artillery.

Ernest Matthews of Nursery Cottages
Durham Light Infantry.

'A Hero of Mons'
George Alfred Hider, Grenadier Guards
Died at Westerham 8th May 1918.

William Pickett of Mill Street
Awarded the Croix de Guerre.

Frederick Chas Paige of Mill Street
Served 5 years in India.

'Westerham Hero'
Joe Cowell of Quebec Square
Awarded the Distinguished Conduct
Medal for conspicuous gallantry on 29th
August 1918.

A Patriotic Westerham Family

L.Corpl. H.W. Hursey
The Queens Regiment.

Pte. Albert Howard
The Queens Regiment
Killed in action on 8th
August 1918.

Pte. Webb
Army Service Corps.

Pte. Harold Howard
Royal Fusiliers.

Corpl. Arthur Chas Mills
Royal Garrison Artillery.

Pte. Herbert Howard
Royal West Kent Regiment.

The sons and sons-in-law of Henry and Phillis Howard
of Springmead, Westerham.

GENERAL WOLFE MEMORIAL, WESTERHAM 2040

Post War, the field gun is displayed beside the Wolfe Statue.

Leading Seaman Archibald Edward Langridge, HMS *Pembroke*

Archibald Edward Langridge joined the Royal Navy as a boy seaman in August 1908. Born at Ightam Mote, Sevenoaks, he had worked as an errand boy before enlisting at the age of 16. He began his training at HMS *Ganges* near Ipswich, where among other duties he became a bugler. His first ship was the cruiser HMS *Berwick*, joining in 1909. He later served in HMS *London* and *Antrim*, and by the outbreak of war in 1914 he was rated a Leading Seaman on the destroyer *Boadicea*. In August 1917 he was paid off from the light cruiser *Penelope*, where he had served for just over a year, and was discharged to the naval barracks at Chatham. The barracks at that time were crowded with new recruits under training and men awaiting drafts to new ships. The accommodation was augmented by using a drill hall as a makeshift dormitory.

On the night of 3/4 September 1917, Langridge and several hundred other sailors were asleep in the crowded drill hall when it was struck by bombs from raiding German aircraft. Over 100 men were killed in the disaster. Leading Seaman Langridge, who had recently married at Westerham and lived at Stakes Cottages, Quebec Square, was among those killed, and is buried at Gillingham.

The air raids in the autumn of 1917 were not totally a cause of alarm and panic. The almost nightly raids on London by Gothas and Zeppelins had brought a spectacle of gun flashes, searchlights and exploding shells that could be viewed from many vantage points looking towards the North Downs. On clear evenings, small crowds of Westerhamers had taken to congregating in the churchyard on the north side of the church where an uninterrupted view of the nightly pyrotechnics could best be obtained. However, on the night of 30 September, the evening's drama took an unexpected turn when shells were seen and heard exploding overhead. Those assembled rapidly dispersed as shell splinters clattered down on nearby roofs. The church service was halted and special constables hurried through the streets ordering people indoors. A decision was taken to close the churchyard at dusk in future and a request was made for an air raid siren.

* * *

The summer and autumn of 1917 would see no relaxation in the fighting on the Western Front. After May 1917 the emphasis of the British effort shifted away from the Arras sector to an area to the south of Ypres in Belgium. Here, at a place called Messines, the army was preparing to dislodge the Germans from a dominant ridge, which they had held since the early battles of 1914. The preparations had been in hand for many months. Vast tunnels and galleries had been excavated extending deep under the German positions. Prior to the planned attack the tunnel heads would be packed with tons of explosive and the tunnels sealed off. Nineteen of these giant mines would be detonated along an enemy front of some six miles. At the same time, British gunners would unleash a ferocious bombardment while the infantry would advance to complete the rout of any of the shaken and terrified enemy who still survived.

At 3.10 a.m. on 7 June 1917, the 19 mines were simultaneously exploded. These shattering detonations literally blew the top off the ridge, destroying the enemy defences and entombing thousands of German soldiers. The explosions were heard across the Channel in southern England as far as London. The attacking troops duly mopped up any enemy soldiers who remained on their feet. The Battle of Messines was one of the few clear-cut victories of the Western Front fighting yet even here the familiar pattern of difficulties in bringing up reserves, advancing beyond artillery support and stiffening enemy resistance meant that there was no breakthrough that could be exploited. The military planners soon turned their attention to fresh pastures.

For most of the war, the small Flemish town of Ypres and its immediate environs was all that remained of Belgian territory in Allied hands. It had been the scene of desperate fighting in 1914 when Britain's small professional army had fought, almost to annihilation, while stemming the German advance on the Channel ports. Since then, the line of a small salient to the east of the town had ebbed and flowed in a series of protracted battles. The terrain of flat fenland and reclaimed polder surrounding Ypres was maintained only by a system of canals and drainage waterways that had been built up over earlier centuries. Any damage to this delicate system would quickly reduce the countryside to lakes of liquefied mud. Moreover, the enemy already controlled any high ground that existed. The British salient at Ypres was overlooked on almost three sides by the German artillery. Yet it was here in the autumn of 1917 that the next phase of the British offensive was planned to take place. What was to become the most controversial and probably the most costly campaign conducted by the British Army commenced at Ypres on 31 July 1917. The object of the attack was to drive out of the existing salient and capture the dominating high ground some five miles to the east. This battle would be officially called the 3rd Battle of Ypres but was more commonly known by the name of the small village that was finally reached at staggering cost some four months later: Passchendaele.

Private Ernest Wood, 2nd/7th Battalion, The Sherwood Foresters

The 2nd/7th Sherwood Foresters were committed to the 3rd Battle of Ypres in September 1917. On the 20th of the month, the battalion marched from the town of Poperinghe, where they had undergone training, and through the ruins of Ypres to enter the trenches east of Wieltje. Serving in the ranks of the Sherwood Foresters was Ernest Wood, age 35, who was born at Westerham. His father Albert Wood had lived at 'Keepers Cottage' adjacent to Big Wood, where he was a gamekeeper for the Squerryes Estate. Ernest Wood was a former employee of the Westerham brewery and at the time of his enlistment, in 1916, his family was living in Lodge Lane, Westerham.

On 26 September 1917, the Sherwood Foresters were part of a general attack on a five-mile front during which the army captured Zonnebeke and Polygon Wood. The war diary of the Sherwood Foresters records that the battalion 'gained and maintained all its objectives in spite of heavy enemy-counter attacks'.

The casualties of the Sherwood Foresters in this operation exceeded 250 killed and wounded. Ernest Wood was among those who died in the attack. He is reported to have been struck in the face by shrapnel and killed instantly. Private Wood is one of the many thousands who died in the battle having no known grave. His name is now recorded on the Tyne Cott Memorial, which stands on the battlefield and commemorates the 'missing' of the Battle of Ypres.

The fighting at Ypres in the months of August, September and October 1917 would test the resolve and endurance of the British Army to the very limit. The terrain, which rapidly turned to a quagmire, and the weather which deteriorated into one of the wettest autumns in history, all conspired to send men into battle soaked, frozen and exhausted even before arriving at the front line. Once there, they were often thrown at fully alerted enemy defences consisting of shell-proof concrete pillboxes, lattices of barbed wire and machine-gun nests. In these attacks men found their weapons jammed with mud while the wounded drowned in shell-holes. These attacks were continued long after any hope of the anticipated 'breakthrough' had passed. By the last week of October the casualties of the Ypres offensive had exceeded 250,000. Yet the army was still only four miles from its start-line and, worse still, the deepening of the salient left the soldiers even more exposed to enemy shellfire.

Many historians would later query how the British soldiers resolve survived the pitiless fighting and the appalling conditions at Ypres in the autumn of 1917. It stands to their eternal credit that no British battalion ever refused to go into the line or refused to go 'over the top'. Their dogged courage and stoical endurance, in the face of what they were asked to do, can only stand as a source of wonderment to later generations. The justification for continuing this appalling battle was the perceived requirement to tie down the German Army and prevent any attack on the French, who were still in some disarray following their disastrous summer offensive. The cost to Britain and the Dominion Armies, however, was prodigious.

On 26 October the troops were prepared for one final assault with the intention of reaching the summit of Passchendaele Ridge. Despite the weather being fine and clear on the preceding day, at midnight, true to form, persistent rain began to fall. At 5.40 a.m. the attack commenced. This day would bring yet more heartbreak for Westerham families.

Private George Walter Allen, 1st Battalion, Royal West Kent Regiment

By late October the 1st Royal West Kents had already suffered badly in the Ypres salient. Entering the trenches astride the Menin Road on 3 October, they endured intense shelling and had driven off several enemy counter-attacks. At 6 a.m. on the 4th they were ordered forward, managing to hold their new positions despite being dreadfully exposed to machine-gun and shellfire. By the time they were relieved, the 1st West Kents had suffered nearly 400 casualties. After a period of rest and intensive training, the battalion once more set out for the front line on 22 October. The depleted ranks had by then been reinforced by drafts from the depot of nearly 350 men. Among the draftees fresh from England was George Walter Allen, age 18, of Mill Street, Westerham.

Allen, a former Hosey boy, would have been no stranger to the war. By the time he enlisted his older brother Alfred, also in the West Kents, had been invalided from Gallipoli and had more recently been wounded in France. By 24 October, the 1st West Kents were back in the same sector on the Menin Road where they had suffered so terribly at the beginning of the month. In the attack of 26 October, launched at 5.40 a.m., the Battalion pressed forward to its objectives across ground resembling a swamp. Many of the West Kents soon found themselves effectively cut off in the German trenches. In a day of great confusion, the persistent enemy counter-attacks eventually drove the surviving West Kents back to their own trenches. By the time they were relieved, the Battalion had suffered a further 300 casualties.

George Walter Allen was killed on this day. His body was never found and he is commemorated on the Tyne Cott Memorial, Ypres.

Lieutenant Colonel Percy William Beresford, 2nd/3rd Battalion, London Regiment

As the 1st Royal West Kents rose from their trenches on the morning of 26 October 1917, the scene was repeated all along the line from the Menin Road to the Houthulst Forest.

Near the village of Poelcapelle, the attacking troops were the 2nd Battalion of the 3rd London Regiment. The 2nd/3rd Londons had arrived at their assembly positions on the 25th with a strength of 15 officers and 616 men under the command of Lieutenant Colonel Percy William Beresford of Westerham.

By October 1917, Beresford was a well-known and much respected citizen of the town. He was born at Twickenham in 1875 and passed through public school and Oxford University before working in a family business. His association with Westerham began when his family took up residence in the town in 1902. After training for the priesthood, Beresford was ordained at Rochester in 1905 and became the curate at St Mary's church. He became closely involved in the community, particularly in founding an Army Cadet Corps, which first paraded in 1904, and was subsequently affiliated with the 1st (Volunteer Battalion) Royal West Kent Regiment.

Through the cadets, Beresford devoted himself to the welfare of local youngsters, becoming an inspirational and much-loved leader as many former cadets would later testify. As an officer in the Territorial Army, he was mobilised in 1914, initially serving with the London Regiment in Malta before moving to France and Flanders. He was wounded at the Battle of Neuve Chapelle in March 1915. He was also awarded the Distinguished Service Order for the action at Bullecourt on 15 May 1917 when his battalion successfully fought off repeated attacks by the Prussian Guard. During this action, Beresford organised assistance to flanking units, which had been temporarily overrun, enabling them to regain their positions. His battalion sustained over 150 casualties in the operation. The 2nd/3rd Londons first fought in the Ypres Salient in August 1917.

On 24 October, the Londons entered the front line, east of Poelcappelle, relieving a battalion of the Middlesex Regiment. The battalion diary states that the move to 'assembly position' was complete by 1 a.m. on the 26th; it also notes the extreme cold and that rain began falling at midnight, continuing until dawn. The Londons advanced to the attack at 5.40 a.m., supported on their flanks by other units of the 58th Division. The appalling ground conditions meant that in some places the men attempted to advance while waist deep in water. The attackers were scourged by enemy machine guns and although some men gained the German positions, they were later forced back by a counter-attack. The survivors of the 2nd/3rd Londons eventually regrouped in their own trenches. The battalion diary states simply, 'our Commanding Officer was mortally wounded during the early morning'.

The melancholy failure of the Londons' attack, so gallantly pressed home in dreadful conditions, was repeated at all points along the line. It is estimated that 12,000 men were lost to no advantage on this day.

The body of Percy Beresford was later recovered and buried near Ypres at Gwalia cemetery, just outside the village of Elverdinge. The news of Beresford's death caused a great sense of shock in Westerham. Flags remained at half-mast at the church and Cadet Headquarters for a week. His sister, who lived at 'The Laurels', London Road, was notified by a War Office telegram on the day following his death. A page of tributes appeared in the *Westerham Herald* recalling his great service to his country and to the town, especially in his leadership of the Westerham Cadets. Two weeks after his death, on Wednesday 7 November, a memorial service was held at St Mary's church commemorating not only the life of Percy Beresford but also remembering the men of Westerham who had already made the supreme sacrifice. The large congregation included officers from the London Regiment, staff and pupils from Westerham schools and representatives of local civic bodies. The Cadet Force, under Captain Cotton, paraded in strength to pay respect to their former leader. The service was led by the Reverend Le Mesurier and an address and tribute given by the Bishop of Rochester. The names of 24 fallen Westerham men were read out to the congregation and after special prayers the service concluded with the singing of 'Abide With Me'.

Yet even as the congregation dispersed, no doubt reflecting on the cost of the war and the sacrifice of so many of its citizens, that total had already increased.

Gunner Henry Arthur Singleton, 91st Brigade, Royal Field Artillery

In the autumn of 1917, at the height of the Battle of Ypres, the men of 91st Brigade, Royal Field Artillery, received some good news. After months of hard fighting and appalling conditions, they were to be withdrawn from the front line and sent to a quiet sector in the Somme region to the south. The batteries fired their last salvoes on 13 October before returning to their wagon lines. On the 18th the whole Brigade – guns and limbers, horses and men – entrained at the town of Proven to the west of Ypres and began the slow journey south. Among the men of A Battery was a young man already a veteran of much fighting and also previously wounded.

Henry Arthur Singleton, age 19, the son of William and Caroline Singleton of New Street, Westerham, had served in France since 1915. Born in Westerham and a Hosey pupil, his was already a military family. At the outbreak of war his elder brother William was already in the Royal Marines and another brother, Albert, was serving in the Royal Navy. In July of the previous year he himself had been wounded in the arm during the Somme offensive. The wound had at least given him some time at home with his family.

Now as the train rumbled south, Henry Singleton and the other gunners must have anticipated some relief away from the Ypres fighting. The next day the Brigade detrained at the town of Peronne near the River Somme and marched to the front line at Sorel.

By 24 October, the Brigade had taken over its new front line sector. During their third day in the line, A Battery came under heavy enemy shellfire, disabling three guns and causing many casualties. Six men, including Gunner Singleton, were killed.

Henry Arthur Singleton is buried at the British cemetery, Sorel-le-Grand.

Westerham's Total War

From a distance of some 90 years, it is hard to comprehend the level of pain and anxiety that was endured by parents like William and Caroline Singleton of New Street during the Great War. By October 1917, their three sons had been away at the war almost from the beginning. Now Henry, who had been wounded the previous year, was killed in action and their eldest son William was again at sea. Another son, Albert, was also serving in the Royal Navy. Every day of those long years these parents lived in hope of the letters from each of their sons stating that all was well and in dread of the official telegram confirming their worst fears. From our own age, where sporting stars are called heroes and stress can mean witnessing an accident, it is hard to appreciate the courage and stoicism of that earlier generation.

Yet the pain and endurance of the Singleton family was being repeated in almost every house in every street in Westerham. The total involvement of some families in the town is truly astonishing. Mr and Mrs J. Cosgrove of Bloomfield Terrace had no less than six sons serving. Mr and Mrs G. Wood of French Street, also had six sons serving, two of whom had been recently wounded. Mr and Mrs Hoath of Southbank had three sons in the army and one in the Royal Marines. The Yorkstons of Madan Road had five sons serving, and Mr and Mrs Salmon of London Road, whose son Nathan had been killed in 1915, had a further three sons serving. The Watts family of Bloomfield Terrace had two sons in the navy, and one in the Australian forces who had been recently gassed at Messines. Mr and Mrs Allen of Mill Street, had one son killed and another wounded and invalided; and two more still serving. The Outrims of Lodge Lane had four sons in the army as did Mrs Phillips of Springfield Cottages. The Haggard and Currie families of 'Breaches', Vicarage Hill, had two serving Brigadier Generals, one Lieutenant Colonel and Lieutenant John Cecil Currie, later to win the Military Cross.

Upward of 10 men from New Street were serving, 8 from Mill

Street, 9 from Southbank and nearly 30 from Madan Road. By the end of 1917 the number of Westerham men in the armed forces had passed 350. In nearly every household in the town a son or husband was away at the war. Firms were stripped of workers and businesses closed down through lack of manpower. To a greater or lesser degree, the war was affecting nearly every family in the town. The following list is of Westerham men wounded in the battles of 1917 and does not include those whose injuries did not justify evacuation to England. The wounds of those listed include multiple shrapnel wounds, bullet wounds, gas poisoning and amputations. The list is not exclusive.

Alfred Allen, Mill Street	Royal West Kents, Shell-shock
Albert Wood, Forge Cottages	Royal West Kents, Bullet wounds
Archibald Ayres, High Street	Royal West Kents, Gassed at Messines
Fred Selby, Madan Road	Royal West Kents, Gunshot wound
Herbert Outrim, Lodge Lane	The Buffs, Gunshot wound
William Sales, Vicarage Hill	Middlesex Regt., Gunshot wound
George Simmons, London Road	East Surreys, Gunshot wound
Walter Wakeford, High Street	Royal Lancaster Regt., Gunshot wound
Harry Bradford, Brewery Cottages	South Lancs. Regt., Gunshot wound
William Wells, Croydon Road	London Regt., Gunshot wound
Wallace Pritchard, Aberdeen House	Australians, Gunshot wound
Arthur Cosgrove, Railway Terrace	Royal Sussex Regt., Gunshot wound
Albert Wood, French Street	Queen's Westminsters, Shoulder wound
Horace Wood, French Street	Royal West Kents, Arm wound

Charles Phillips, Springfield Cotts	Royal Warwicks, Leg amputation
William Keely, Madan Road	Royal Fusiliers, Gas poisoning
Albert Watts, Bloomfield Terrace	Australians, Gas poisoning
Harold Verrall, The Forge	Honourable Artillery Company, Trench foot
Arthur Streatfield, Mill Cottages	Royal West Kents, Invalided from India
William Hoath, High Street	Royal West Kents, Invalided from India
George Whitmore, The Crown	Royal West Kents, Invalided from India

By November 1917, Mrs Leney of New Street still had no news of her husband, missing at Arras since April. Mrs Terry of Hosey also waited for news of her husband Charles, missing in the same battle. For Westerham families the news from every quarter was cause for concern or heartbreak. It was about to get considerably worse.

The Battle of Cambrai

Even as the great Ypres offensive of 1917 was withering away in the mud and desolation in front of Passchendaele, plans were already afoot for a new British attack. This attack would take place in the south, near to the old Somme battlefield. The assault would be directly against the German Hindenburg Line and would also employ the recently developed tracked fighting vehicle, the tank.

First used in battle in 1916, tanks had been employed in small numbers in support of infantry attacks. This time, with several hundred of the new vehicles available, the tank would be the primary weapon. Other operational innovations being employed would be the total secrecy of the mobilisation and the absence of any preliminary bombardment giving notice of an attack. The assault was scheduled for the morning of 20 November 1917 and would be launched towards the town and important railhead of Cambrai, some five miles distant. Among the units committed to the battle was the 56th (Territorial) London Division, which included the 1st Battalion, The London Scottish.

The London Scottish was originally a Territorial Army unit formed from expatriate Scotsmen living in the capital but, by late 1917, its ranks had been diluted with draftees and returning wounded from a host of other regiments. However, it still sought to maintain its Scots identity by, among other things, the wearing of the kilt. The Adjutant of the London Scots, Captain Allen Grant Douglas, was a son of the Westerham family, Major and Mrs W.J. Douglas of Farley House. Also in the ranks of the battalion was another Westerham soldier, John Christopher Lander.

Private John Christopher Lander, 1st/14th Battalion, London Regiment (The London Scottish)

The initial attack by the tanks at Cambrai had gone extremely well. Total surprise had been achieved and the supporting infantry had the comparatively easy task of mopping up outposts of demoralised Germans. However, in the days that followed, the resistance stiffened and many tanks became disabled, ditched or destroyed by enemy action. The 56th London Division came into the line on the extreme left of the battle front and on 23 November the London Scottish were ordered forward to continue the attack.

Private John Lander, aged 23, was among the troops detailed to assault a German trench system code named 'Tadpole Lane'. Amid great confusion and fierce fighting, the London Scottish gained their objectives during the 23rd but on the following day they were subjected to a heavy bombardment, which preceded an enemy counter-attack. During the 24th, the London Scots were forced back to their own lines, suffering further heavy casualties. Private Lander was among those killed in the fighting of 23 November. In a letter of condolence to his parents, the commanding officer stated that Private Lander would be recommended for an award for his gallantry on the day he died. Sadly, this appears not to have materialised.

John Lander, who was the son of John and Carrie Lander of Betsom's Hill Farm, Westerham, has no known grave and is commemorated on the Cambrai Memorial, France.

Despite the initial success of the opening attack, by 26 November the British forces were still some way short of their objectives of the first day. Fighting had become centred on the strategically important position of Bourlon Wood, which controlled the main line of advance to Cambrai. The 51st (Highland) Division, which had been fighting almost continuously since the beginning of the battle, was withdrawn, being relieved by troops of the newly-arrived Guards Division. Among the battalions of Scots, Irish and Coldstream Guards of the Guards Division were the 3rd Battalion, Grenadier Guards, and serving in the ranks of the Grenadiers was a former Hosey boy, Jack Knight, whose parents, James and Martha, lived in Madan Road, Westerham.

Private James Walter (Jack) Knight, 3rd Battalion, Grenadier Guards

On the day following their arrival in the front line, the Guards Division was ordered to renew the attack on the Bourlon Wood position. At 6.20 a.m. on 27 November, the 3rd Grenadiers, flanked by Scots and Coldstream Guards and assisted by a number of tanks, began the assault. Almost immediately there were casualties to artillery and machine-gun fire. The Guards Division history records that desperate fighting continued all day on the edge of Bourlon Wood and in the ruins of the nearby village of Fontaine. Two companies of Grenadiers were almost wiped out in the assault. The arrival of strong German reinforcements left the surviving guardsmen almost isolated in the enemy lines. The Guards fought desperately against being surrounded and eventually retreated under covering fire. The casualties of the Guards Division exceeded 1,000 killed, wounded and missing. Jack Knight was among those who were listed as missing in the battle of 27 November – he was never heard of again.

The day of 27 November 1917 marked the end of the British offensive at Cambrai. The troops dug in where the fighting had ended and attempted to consolidate their gains. The British had driven a wedge into the German lines at great cost, but it was calculated that the enemy had also lost heavily and were considered in no position to mount a counter-stroke. Unbeknown to the British, the Germans were already planning a stunning riposte.

It was delivered just three days later, on Friday 30 November.

Captain Allen Grant Douglas, 1st/14th Battalion, London Regiment (The London Scottish)

During the savage fighting of 27 November, the 1st/14th Londons had been held in reserve, but moved up to the front line that evening to positions they had occupied earlier in the battle. By November 1917 the London Scottish had already seen much active service. Its men had been the first Territorial unit to fight in France back in November 1914 and had served throughout the Somme campaign of the previous year. Few of its original members now survived.

The adjutant of the London Scots, Captain Allen Grant Douglas, had been with the Battalion since October 1915. Douglas was a veteran of much fighting and had been awarded the Military Cross for gallantry during the Battle of Arras in April 1917. The Douglas family had moved to Westerham in 1915, taking up residence at Farley House, having originally lived at Bickley, Kent. Allen Grant Douglas had been educated at Rugby School and later studied marine engineering. His father, Major William Douglas, was a naval architect and served with the Allied command in France during the war. His mother, Ada Douglas, had become an active community member while living in Westerham, working with many local organisations.

Now, during 28 and 29 November 1917, the London Scots at Cambrai strove to strengthen their positions by continual digging and wiring. On the morning of 30

92

November, it was obvious that something was afoot. Enemy shelling intensified and troops were seen massing across no man's land, preparing to attack. At 7.30 a.m., all along the line of the Cambrai salient, the Germans pressed home their assault, achieving astonishing success in the south by driving in the British line to a depth of three miles. All day the London Scots were engaged in beating off enemy assaults. By the time they were relieved, the Battalion had suffered over 300 casualties. Allen Grant Douglas was killed in action while organising the London Scots' defence which, despite repeated attacks, had not yielded an inch of ground. One report stated that Captain Douglas had been hit in the head and died instantly. He is buried nearby at the village of Moeuvres, a mile west of Bourlon Wood. A memorial service for Douglas was held in December at the parish church at Bickley, Kent.

Although the Germans recovered some of their lost territory during the counter-attack, the line eventually stabilised and both sides dug in for the winter. The Battle of Cambrai had cost the lives of three Westerham soldiers in less than six days.

* * *

As 1917 drew to a close, Westerham faced another sombre wartime Christmas. Despite the agricultural emphasis of local industry, many basic foodstuffs were now in short supply. The depredation by enemy submarines had severely restricted imported food and rationing was now in force for many commodities. Cards were issued by the Food Committee, without which sugar could not be bought, and coal restrictions were also in place. Clothing could also only be bought by 'card' from registered drapers. Prior to Christmas, parcels were once again handed in at the vicarage for onward dispatch to Westerham men serving at the Front.

Throughout 1917 the Westerham Cadet Corps had been extremely active and, in December, a bugle band was formed.

Under their leader, Captain Cotton, the Westerham and Chipstead Corps mustered 113 cadets. At the recent annual inspection, at which General Currie of 'Breaches' presented awards, it was noted that from the many old cadets now serving in the forces, 7 had gained commissions while no less than 13 had made the supreme sacrifice. The enthusiasm of the Cadet Corps appeared to increase as the war intensified.

Three days before Christmas, heavy snowfalls caused drifting which closed a number of local roads. The 'Rips' between Westerham and Limpsfield was impassable and Westerham Hill and Tatsfield were cut off. Also at Christmas, Westerhamers were informed that food shops would be closed for three days over the festive period. This was more a reflection of restricted supplies rather than the need for an extended holiday. Mr Boddy announced that his butcher shop would close and not reopen until further supplies could be obtained. On Christmas Day, the usual church services were held at St Mary's, at which the collections were donated to the sick and poor of the parish.

1918

As 1917 ended and 1918 began, it seemed that the news from every quarter was uniformly bad. The fighting in Flanders, which ended in November, had brought only horrendous casualties with little to show for all the effort and sacrifice. The Battle of Cambrai, which initially gave hopes of a real victory, had also petered out in the all too familiar stalemate. These battles during the autumn of 1917 had cost the town of Westerham no less than seven of its citizens killed and at least 15 seriously wounded.

On the international front, the Italians had suffered a severe defeat at the hands of the Austrians at Caporetto while Russia had been forced out of the war altogether by a revolution at home. A peace deal was even then being dictated, which would enable Germany to transfer a million of its troops from the Eastern to the Western Front. The Allied armies in France would soon have to brace themselves for the inevitable onslaught that would be launched as soon as the German armies in the west had been sufficiently reinforced. For the Germans this offensive would dictate the outcome of the entire war. They would have to win the war in the spring of 1918 before the arrival of American troops swung the balance decisively in the Allies' favour. The entry of America into the war in 1917 was a great boost to the Allies but it would take time for US armies to arrive and become effective.

At home, the war was affecting nearly every aspect of life. Men were away at the Front, commodities of all descriptions were in short supply and all kinds of foodstuffs were becoming scarce and subject to controls. In Westerham, the shortages resulted in food cards being issued to every household (ration books to a later generation) and registration was required at all food shops. As a means of supplementing the meagre diet, all kinds of innovative practices were adopted. A Rabbit Club was formed, so that any baby rabbits could be pooled among members, and lectures on poultry-keeping were given at the Men's Club. A Pig Club also came into being – anyone with spare land or space on an allotment was urged to consider keeping a pig as an efficient way of creating meat out of swill and leftovers. As the crisis deepened, the parish council met under Mr Shawyer to consider the viability of communal kitchens – already a fact of life in some parts of London. It was agreed that, as a minimum, more land was required for the provision of allotments. An area at the back of the Warde Arms was suggested.

Elsewhere in the town, paper salvage was being collected in earnest and the National Service Committee's workroom still kept up a prodigious output of socks, mufflers and other knitwear for men at the Front. A selection of thank-you letters was printed in the *Herald* from Westerham soldiers in receipt of the Christmas parcels dispatched from the vicarage. Letters were received from Peter Barnett of the West Kents, William Gooding of the Engineers, Fred Shergold of the RAMC, Harry Cosgrove of the West Kents and Frank Jarrett, Royal Engineers. A letter was also received from Fred Baker, Royal Artillery, expressing his thanks despite the parcel's non-arrival. His parcel was languishing somewhere in France while he was recovering from gas poisoning at a hospital in Scotland.

January 1918 found many of the Westerham men in France enduring miserable conditions. Archibald Ayres, with the 7th West Kents, was in the mud and desolation of the Ypres salient; Horace Martin, from Madan Road, with the 6th West Kents was in the line on the River Lys near the Belgian border, and the twice wounded William Hayward was now working with a Labour Company. On the other side of no man's land, a steady build up of forces continued as a million German soldiers, now released from the Russian front, moved westwards.

For the men of the 1st Battalion, Royal West Kents, the New Year opened in slightly more pleasant surroundings. In December 1917 they had been rushed to Italy to help shore up the defences after the Austrian breakthrough. January found them in the front line on the River Piave. Also with the British forces dispatched to Italy were the 10th Battalion, The Queen's

Regiment, and serving in the ranks was a young Westerham soldier, Sydney Charles King.

Private Sydney Charles King, 10th Battalion, The Queen's (Royal West Surrey Regiment)

The Italian collapse at Caporetto in late 1917 had caused great alarm in the Allied high command. In a matter of a few days the battle in north-east Italy had resulted in the Italian Army retreating some 80 miles and losing over 250,000 prisoners to the victorious Austro-German armies. Despite the critical situation on the Western Front, four British divisions were immediately dispatched to Italy.

The men of the 10th Battalion, Queen's Royal West Surreys, were among those who in late November 1917 found themselves enjoying a remarkable change of scenery. After entraining near Ypres, the 10th Queen's began a five-day journey to northern Italy, taking in the coastline of the French and Italian Rivieras. Delays and congestion on the line meant that there were frequent stops enabling the troops to sample local hospitality along the route and return to the journey laden with fruit, wine and other long-forgotten delights.

Sydney Charles King of New Street, Westerham, had scarcely been of age when he enlisted in 1914. A former Hosey boy and a member of the Cadets, he joined the Queen's Royal West Surreys at Croydon on the outbreak of war and was posted to one of the new service battalions of the regiment. He landed in France with his battalion on 27 July 1915. In 1916, he was wounded during the Battle of the Somme, receiving gunshot wounds in the knee from which he was invalided home. Following his recovery, he returned to France to serve with the regiments 10th Battalion. The 10th Queen's later endured the long agony of the 3rd Battle of Ypres from August 1917.

Now in late November 1917, as the train meandered its way along the spectacular Mediterranean coastline, the troops must have anticipated a better destination than the mud and desolation they had left behind in Belgium. By 4 December, the newly-arrived British troops began taking over positions on the recently stabilised front line near the River Piave. Here they returned to the all too familiar routine of trench warfare and 'turns' in the line. In the first week of January 1918, the battalion was in the trenches on the Montello sector, near the town of Giavera, enduring extreme cold and occasional enemy shelling. Private King was mortally wounded during this period, succumbing to his wounds on 7 January. Sydney Charles King died aged 21 and was the son of Edmund and Emma King of New Street, Westerham. He is buried at Giavera British cemetery, Italy.

The losses incurred in the Ypres offensive of the preceding autumn had caused a manpower crisis in the British Expeditionary Force. Not only had the casualty deficiencies not been made good, but the army was also required to extend its line in the south, taking over sectors previously held by the French Army. A radical expedient was devised in early 1918 whereby each infantry brigade was reduced by one battalion from four to three. Many of the battalions raised to great fanfare at the beginning of the war now passed quietly away, the released men being used to make up the strength of the remaining units. Where possible the released men were used to reinforce other battalions of their own regiment but this was not always the case. Among the 153 battalions disbanded in February 1918 was the 3rd/4th Royal West Kents who had been in France since the previous summer. They had served at Ypres during the great offensive and spent the winter taking turns in the trenches at Cambrai. Now the Battalion's personnel were dispersed to other battalions, around 200 men being transferred to the 7th Battalion of the parent regiment.

Sergeant Charles Albert Bateman, 7th Battalion, Royal West Kent Regiment

The 7th Battalion, Royal West Kents had suffered grievously during the battles at Ypres and Passchendaele in late 1917, and had begun the New Year well under strength. In February 1918, the newly-arrived contingent from the disbanded 3rd/4th Battalion had gone some way to make good the losses. But the newcomers had barely time to bed in before the Battalion was required to brace itself for the next anticipated struggle.

In March 1918, the 7th RWKs found themselves in a sector recently taken over from the French Army, just a few miles south of the town of St Quentin. The Battalion had little time to prepare and strengthen its defensive positions ahead of the major German attack that all agreed was now imminent. Among the men of the old 3rd/4th who were now hastily adapting themselves to new surroundings and a different unit was 20-year-old Sergeant Charles Albert Bateman of London Road, Westerham.

Bateman was the third son of Frederick Bateman who was a foreman gardener at the London Road nursery. The family home was nearby at 2 Nursery Cottages. Although born at Sidcup where his family lived for some time, Charles Bateman belonged to the Bateman's of Horns Hill, Westerham, where his father and grandfather were born. In common with most local youngsters, he attended Hosey School and was a member of the Army Cadets. In June 1914, aged 17, he moved from the Cadets to the Territorials.

At the outbreak of war, being too young for overseas service, Charles remained with the home service contingent when the 1st/4th RWKs were sent to India. After the 2nd/4th Battalion was sent overseas in 1915, he remained with the newly-designated 3rd/4th Battalion which was constituted for war service in July of the same year. After long periods on standby, based at Canterbury, the 3rd/4th RWKs landed in France on 1 June 1917. The 3rd/4th's initiation in trench warfare began at Arras, followed by periods in the Ypres sector where the battalion acted as 'Pioneers'. The winter of 1917 was spent in and out of the line near Cambrai before the disbandment order in early 1918 dispersed the men to other units.

On 20 March 1918, Charles Bateman was near the village of Moy, just south of St Quentin, still striving to improve the defences ahead of the anticipated German assault. The line at this point did not consist of a continuous trench system but relied on defensive redoubts with overlapping fire zones. The shortcomings of this system were soon apparent when thick fog began to form on the night of 20 March.

During the night, reports were circulated that enemy troops were massing and that the attack was imminent. At 4.30 a.m. on the 21st, an intense bombardment was opened all along the British front. High explosive and gas shells rained down on the West Kents' positions causing massive destruction and casualties. As dawn approached, an attack by waves of German infantry developed. With fog restricting visibility to 30 yards, the attackers were able to infiltrate and pass behind the West Kents' positions. Despite heroic resistance, many of the defensive redoubts were soon cut off. Some of these posts fought on until overwhelmed while others surrendered when it was realised they were isolated and well behind the line of the German advance.

The 7th Royal West Kents were all but annihilated on 21 March 1918, and Sergeant Bateman was among those listed as missing. All those killed, wounded or missing on 21 March were left behind in the German advance, which penetrated the British lines by up to 20 miles over the coming days. A letter from a comrade to Charles Bateman's parents stated that he had been wounded in the head and was reported killed. The hope remained that he was among those taken prisoner but nothing further was ever heard of his fate. Charles Albert Bateman is assumed to have been killed in action. He is now named on the Pozieres Memorial, France that lists the names of 20,000 men 'missing' in the battles of early 1918.

In the 7th Royal West Kents' action of 21 March, another Westerham soldier was reported missing. Archibald Ayres, whose parents lived in the High Street, was later confirmed as a prisoner of war, spending the next eight months in Germany.

The German attack of March 1918 achieved what no other offensive had accomplished in the war so far – a complete breakthrough. The area of the old Somme battlefield, gained at enormous cost in 1916, was given up in a matter of days and at its furthest point the Germans advance reached 35 miles before exhaustion, lack of supplies and the stiffening Allied resistance caused the line to stabilise. Yet, impressive as the advance may have been, it was achieved at a cost the Germans could ill afford. Their casualties after nearly four years of fighting could not easily be replaced. Moreover, it proved that gaining a few square miles of shell-torn wilderness did not necessarily constitute a victory any more than giving up ground of no strategic importance equalled defeat. The German spring offensive would finally run its course by the early summer of 1918, after which it would be the Allies who would resume the offensive. Before that, however, there would be much hard fighting and more heartbreak for Westerham families.

Bombardier John Whitebread, Royal Garrison Artillery

John Whitebread was born at Sundridge, Kent, in 1887, the son of George and Sarah. In March 1901 the family lived in Westerham at Church Alley, off Vicarage Hill. At the age of 13, John is recorded as working as a general labourer. Prior to 1914 he lived and worked in the

Shortlands area of Bromley before enlisting in the Artillery in December 1915. He served with the 151st Siege Battery, Royal Garrison Artillery, the army's heavy gunners. In the German offensive of 21 March 1918, Whitebread was near to the town of Arras where the attack was largely contained thanks to better-prepared defences. The following days still saw much heavy fighting in the Arras sector as the Germans sought to capture the important town. John Whitebread was killed in action on 28 March while his battery was engaged in this desperate battle. He is buried on the western outskirts of Arras at Fauburg D'Amiens cemetery.

Private Alfred Ernest Wood,
9th Battalion, Norfolk Regiment

By April 1918, George and Mary Wood of French Street, Westerham were certainly no strangers to the war. Six of their sons were now in uniform, two of whom had been wounded during the previous year. Horace Wood, serving with the Royal West Kents, had been wounded in the hand and Albert, in the Queen's Westminster Rifles, was wounded in the right shoulder. With three more sons away at the Front, the news of the renewed heavy fighting in France was cause for unimaginable anxiety in the Wood household.

Alfred Ernest Wood, the second youngest son, aged 18, had only recently joined the Royal West Kents. Along with many newly-recruited youngsters, he would have been retained at home until his nineteenth birthday, but the crisis of early 1918 meant that large numbers of these young soldiers were quickly drafted to France. Many would find themselves sent away from their own regiment to make up losses wherever they were needed.

In April 1918, Alfred was serving in the 9th Norfolks at Ypres. It was in this sector that the Germans launched the next phase of their spring offensive. The April offensive in Flanders was another critical battle for the Allies, causing enormous casualties on both sides. On 15 April, the 9th Norfolks were attacked in their trenches near Ypres and were eventually forced to withdraw towards Kemmel.

Alfred Wood was among those killed in action that day and is one of the many whose body was never recovered. His name is listed on the Tyne Cott Memorial, Zonnebeke, Flanders.

Sapper William Stanley Gooding, 255th Tunnelling Company, Royal Engineers

To the infantrymen in the front line it often seemed that those in the supporting services had a much easier time. The Army Service Corps who brought up the supplies and ammunition, the Royal Army Medical Corps who attended the wounded and the Royal Engineers who built roads and ran telephone cables, all seemed for the most part to have a life of comparative safety if not of comfort. Although this impression may be understandable, it was far from being strictly accurate. All areas close to the front line were subject to shelling with road junctions, troop concentrations and supply dumps always being sought by the enemy artillery. Shellfire was particularly devastating to horse-drawn transport which had no chance of taking cover and suffered terribly as a consequence. The men of the Medical Corps often attended the wounded under fire, and the repair and relaying of telephone cables frequently required engineers to be exposed to mortar and sniper fire, sometimes in broad daylight. Among the most daunting and perilous duties was that of specialist companies of Royal Engineers employed in the digging of mine shafts that extended under the German lines. When completed, the ends of the shafts were packed with explosives to be later detonated with devastating consequences for the Germans manning the trenches above. Both sides were engaged in mining warfare, often in the same vicinity. Sometimes opposing shafts would break into each other, resulting in desperate underground grenade and firefights. When enemy countermining was suspected, the tunnellers constantly paused to listen for sounds of digging. The tension among the men engaged in this kind of warfare, against the constant fear of being buried alive, defies the imagination.

The 255th Tunnelling Company, Royal Engineers, was one the army's units employed in this work. The 255th had been involved in mining and fortification work at Neuville St Vaast and Vimy Ridge in 1917 but had later moved to the Ypres sector. In the summer of 1918 they had been attached to the French Army and were assisting with strengthening defences near the village of Boeschepe. Here, new trenches were dug and existing ones rewired. Many of the men in the tunnelling companies were miners in civilian life but the ranks of the 255th included Sapper William Stanley Gooding of South Bank, Westerham.

Gooding was born at Four Elms in 1882. He later lived with grandparents at Crockham Hill where his occupation is listed as an artist and signwriter. By the time of enlisting in the Royal Engineers in 1916, he was married to Agnes Gooding and was residing at 11 South Bank, Westerham.

On the night of 30 May 1918, the tunnellers were withdrawn to tented billets near Abeele. During that night the camp came under artillery fire, which killed 35 men of the Company. The following day the survivors had the unenviable task of burying their dead comrades. Sapper Gooding, aged 37, was among those killed. He is buried at Lijssenthoek Military cemetry near Ypres, Belgium. His daughter, Mrs Anne Ring, is still a Westerham resident.

When the fighting line stabilised in the summer of 1918, it was due as much to the exhaustion of the opposing armies as to any other cause. The Germans had failed in their bid to defeat the Allies but the cost on both sides had been prodigious. Besides the five Westerham men killed since the beginning of the year, at least four had been seriously wounded and five others had become prisoners of war. Charles Jupp of London Road, whose father was with the West Kents in the Middle East, was wounded while serving with the West Yorkshire Regiment. Percy Darlington of the Royal Welsh Fusiliers, whose family lived at 'Well House', was severely wounded by a grenade. Clifford Selby from Madan Road, of the Essex Regiment, suffered gas poisoning and his two other brothers were also at the Front. Fred Yorkston, also of Madan Road, who had spent seven months recovering from wounds from the Somme, had endured almost continual fighting since March 1918. In May, his battalion, the 2nd Rifle Brigade, had been withdrawn from the battle and sent to a 'quiet' sector on the River Aisne. Four days after their arrival, on 27 May, the Germans launched the next phase of their offensive on this very area. Wounded by a grenade, Yorkston spent the rest of the war in Germany.

Other Westerham men captured in the spring offensive were Harold Hatcher of New Street (South Lancashire Regiment), George Wood of Railway Terrace (Royal West Kents) and George Hall of Madan Road, (1st Wiltshires). Another Westerham family, the Pritchards of Aberdeen House, received disquieting news of their son, Lieutenant Wallace Pritchard of the Australian Infantry. On 3 May he was wounded for the third time in the war, this time losing two fingers of his right hand and receiving a severe bullet wound to the leg. Second Lieutenant Frank Newton of the 11th Hampshire Regiment, whose family lived at 'Bincleaves', was also reported wounded on 30 March.

In Westerham, during the summer of 1918, the news from all quarters seemed uniformly bad. On the home front, the food and fuel crisis had given rise to all kinds of measures to help alleviate the shortages. Jam sales were held at the Drill Hall, the Rabbit

105

Club held markets at the Men's Club and the Pig Club met to arrange bulk buying of feed. More allotments were made available at Madan Road and a limited supply of sugar was sold for jam-making. Coke from the Croydon Road gas works became subject to rationing while the parish council still discussed the viability of communal kitchens.

Despite the sombre background, the output of the National Service Committee workshop continued to break all records. By the middle of 1918 an incredible 11,000 knitted articles had been produced and dispatched to soldiers at the Front. Concerts, whist drives and other entertainment still continued at St Mary's Hall, although dances were suspended while the crisis in France continued. As more young men reached the age of 18, they immediately became eligible for conscription. Oxted and Sevenoaks tribunals still heard appeals against call-up. Typical of the claims heard were: 'last butcher in the village', 'only worker left on the farm' and 'maintains water supply for the estate'. Exemptions were often granted but usually with a limit of two or three months.

Cruel though the war may have been to the townspeople of Westerham, they lived in an age when early death was sadly not uncommon. Infant mortality, from a host of diseases that are now eradicated, was very much a fact of life and the sudden tragic death of an adult, apparently in the prime of life, was a constant reminder of human frailty. In an age of relatively primitive mechanisation, industrial accidents at farms and other workplaces also regularly claimed lives. In the period when three Westerham soldiers were killed at Ypres in 1917, two men also lost their lives in local working accidents. The casualty lists of the First World War contain a surprising proportion of men having died from causes other than enemy action. Six of those named on the Westerham war memorial died from non-military causes. While some of these deaths were no doubt exacerbated by military service, it was also a reflection of the more rigorous times in which people lived. While tragic death may have been no more acceptable than it is today, it was sadly far more commonplace.

106

Private George Alfred Hider, 2nd Battalion, Grenadier Guards

George Alfred Hider was born at Ightham, Sevenoaks, in 1880. On leaving school he worked as a bricklayer's labourer before enlisting in the Grenadier Guards in November 1905. He served in the Grenadiers on home service for three years before transferring to the Reserve. In 1908 he returned to his former employment, working in the Sevenoaks area and in 1910 he was married to Ellen Smith of Kemsing. The Hiders moved to Westerham prior to the First World War, where they lived at Horseman's Cottage, London Road. They had a son and two daughters. While living in Westerham, George worked as a postman.

On the outbreak of war he was immediately recalled. Within a week of returning to the Guards' barracks in London, George was mobilised and kitted out for war, landing in France on 13 August. Over the next six months the 2nd Grenadiers fought from Mons to the River Aisne and later in the 1st Battle of Ypres. The Grenadiers endured the dreadful winter of 1915 in the trenches near Ypres.

George first reported sick with chest pains in February 1915. In April he spent three days at a base hospital before being placed on light duties. When his symptoms persisted, he was sent to hospital in England on 4 June, where he was diagnosed with a tumour. The medical board considered his condition was 'not caused, but aggravated by active service'. He was discharged from the army, no longer fit for military service, on 30 August 1915.

George returned to his old job as a Westerham postman until deteriorating health eventually forced his retirement. He died, aged 38, on 8 May 1918 and was buried in St Mary's churchyard. His grave is marked by a War Graves headstone, which reads:

Private G.A. Hider, Grenadier Guards

Died 8.5.1918.

At its peak in 1917, the number of horses employed by the British Army in France exceeded half a million, a number that was supplemented by around a quarter of a million mules. The support required for this colossal number of animals was vast. Some estimates place the forage requirement for this equine population as utilising a quarter of all the shipping between England and France. The horses were by no means only the preserve of the cavalry. All artillery units required horses, not only to transport the guns but for the constant supply of ammunition. Horse-drawn wagons were used extensively for bringing supplies to the front line and where mud or difficult terrain dictated, pack mules were employed for the same purpose. Even infantry units were allocated horses to be used in a variety of tasks. The use of mechanical transport was limited in the early part of the war and largely unreliable before 1918.

The demand for horses was such that many were purchased and shipped from as far afield as Argentina and America. Inevitably, the animals suffered terribly in the course of the fighting. At least half of all the horses and mules dispatched to France were killed or died as a result of war service. Men with experience of horses in civilian life were often employed in the care and welfare of the animals. Base depots were set up at French Channel ports to attend to transiting horses and to allocate horses to front line units as required. Sick or maimed animals were returned to these depots for assessment as to their curability or otherwise. The 9th Veterinary Hospital of the Royal Army Veterinary Corps had been established at the French port of Dieppe in 1915. On the staff since 1915 was Private H.D. Penicard, lately of Westerham.

Private Harry Denis Pennicard, Army Veterinary Corps

Harry Denis Pennicard was born at Kirdford, near Billingshurst, Sussex in 1884. For some years prior to 1914, he and his wife Edith had worked in the service of the Reverend Henry Bartlett at 'Farley Croft', Westerham.

He volunteered for the army in 1914 and served in France from 5 January 1915. Over the following years, thousands of animals passed through the 9th Veterinary Hospital depot.

In the spring and early summer of 1918, Europe lay in the grip of an epidemic of Spanish flu. Armies in France, on both sides, were badly affected by the outbreak, and the close confines in which men lived and fought ensured a rapid spread of the disease. In most cases men recovered with rest and care but some were not so fortunate. Where individuals were already laid low by fatigue and poor diet, complications often set in. Harry Pennicard was among those afflicted where the condition turned to pneumonia. While still at Dieppe, he died from the disease on 11 June 1918. He is buried at Janval cemetery, Dieppe, France.

By the time the German spring offensive had run its course in the summer of 1918, the 6th Royal West Kents had been fighting almost continuously for three months. When the attack began on 21 March, the Battalion had been hurried down from the north and had taken up a position near the town of Albert on the edge of the old 1916 Somme battlefield. Here, in desperate fighting over many weeks, the German advance was gradually brought to a standstill. By mid-June the exhausted German Army was trying to consolidate its gains while the British regrouped and made plans to drive them out.

Private Charles Henry Horace Martin, 6th Battalion Royal West Kents

The 6th Battalion, Royal West Kents, had been drawn to the Somme fighting at the end of the March 1918. After helping to stem the German advance in April, the Battalion remained in the vicinity of Albert through May and June, taking turns in the trenches near the village of Bouzincourt.

For Private Horace Martin of B Company, the latest fighting was a continuation of a long and active war. Born at Cranbrook in 1894, he had lived at Westerham with his family most of his life, first in Rysted Lane and latterly at 'The Larches', Madan Road. His father, Harry Martin, had been a long-standing member of the local Volunteer Battalion. Horace attended Hosey School and was also a former cadet. He was mobilised with the Territorials at the outbreak of war and served in France from sometime in 1916. The 6th Royal West Kents fought on the Somme in 1916 and again at Arras in 1917.

In the later stages of the Battle of Arras the Battalion took part in a local attack near Monchy-le-Preux. In this action, on 17 July 1917, Private Martin was part of a small group who found themselves cut off and surrounded in the enemy trenches. Under the command of an officer, the small detachment of West Kents held out until nightfall when they were relieved by a further advance. In a letter to his parents, Private Martin describes in sprightly terms how he later volunteered to take a message back across no man's land to the battalion HQ where the colonel received him with great enthusiasm. Private Martin was awarded the Military Medal for his conduct on that day.

The 6th Battalion also fought at Cambrai in November 1917 before their arrival on the Somme in the spring of 1918. Now, on 30 June, the 6th Royal West Kents were once again detailed to attack. Their objective this time was small tactical position opposite their trenches at Bouzincourt. At 9.35 p.m., the men went over the top, supported by a barrage of artillery and machine-gun fire. The enemy front line was quickly taken but as the attackers pressed on there was sharp fighting and resistance was encountered. By the time the objectives had been gained, the Battalion had suffered severe casualties amounting to some 230 men killed and wounded. Private Martin was among those missing in the attack. Later, when the tide of war moved further east, his body was eventually found. Private Martin died aged 24, and was buried close to the battlefield at Harponville, France

By the summer of 1918, the German attacks that commenced on 21 March had finally run their course. The British and French Armies had been pushed back on a number of fronts from Ypres to the River Marne, in some places to a depth of 40 miles, but the line had not broken.

Now it was the Allies that considered their options. For the British Army, the beginning of August 1918 marked the fourth anniversary of its arrival in France. The small expeditionary force of five divisions that had landed in August 1914 had now grown to one of awesome proportions. From an army that moved by horse and foot with cavalry armed with sword and lance, within four years it had become a force that is recognisable in the present century. Now it possessed a Tank Corps with 500 battle tanks and smaller armoured vehicles, an air arm proficient in artillery spotting and ground support, mechanised infantry and an independent Machine Gun Corps, all incorporating a host of technical innovations from radio command to chemical warfare. In France alone there were over 50 fighting divisions.

For the Germans, exhausted after their attacks in March to May, the situation was increasingly bleak. With little reserve of manpower and starved of food and raw materials by the Royal Navy blockade, they could only await the Allied onslaught. America's entry into the war in 1917 with its potential of almost unlimited manpower only emphasised German isolation. The coming Allied offensive would not be straightforward. The Germans were still capable of fierce resistance and the casualties caused would be as severe as at any period of the war, but the attack would be decisive.

The blow was finally delivered on 8 August 1918.

Private Albert Charles Howard, 7th Battalion, The Queen's Royal West Surrey Regiment

Albert Charles Howard was the son of Henry and Phyllis Howard of Springfield Cottages, Westerham. Henry Howard worked as a local blacksmith and had a family of four sons and three daughters. Albert, the second youngest, was born in 1897. In common with many Westerham youngsters he made his way via Hosey School and the Army Cadets into the Territorials of the 4th Royal West Kents. His main occupation on leaving school was an assistant at Mr Shawyer's general stores in the market square.

In August 1914, he was mobilised with his battalion and was later among those dispatched to India with the 1st/4th Battalion. Although the 1st/4th Royal West Kents spent the entire war in India, a number of its younger personnel were brought home to serve in other theatres, being replaced by older soldiers more suited to garrison duty. Albert returned from India in 1916 and was posted to the Queen's Royal West Surreys.

By the time he was sent to France in 1918, two of his brothers were also serving; Harold in the Kings Royal Rifle Corps and Herbert in the Royal West Kents. Herbert had been wounded in France during the previous year and had spent some time recovering in England. In August 1918, Albert was a few miles east of Amiens, France, where the fighting line had stabilised some months earlier.

On 7 August, as part of the general British advance, the Battalion moved forward to its assembly positions just short of the German line. At 4.30 a.m. on 8 August, the 7th Queen's attacked astride the road between the villages of Bray and Corbie. The Battalion diary mentions casualties to enemy bombardment, and describes the commanding officer going forward to deal with the situation, gathering all available men, and leading them on to their objective. The day's fighting was a tremendous success for the British Army. Within a matter of days the Germans were being driven back across the old Somme battlefield. The Germans were later to describe 8 August as the 'Black Day'.

For the 7th Queen's, it had been a day of hard fighting with heavy casualties. Private Howard, aged 21, was among those missing after the action. His body was never found. He is now named on the Vis-en-Artois Memorial, which commemorates those soldiers listed as missing in the period beginning 8 August 1918, a time that became known as the 'Advance to Victory'.

The main thrust of the attacks that began on 8 August had been entrusted to the Dominion Army divisions of Australia and Canada. Attacking south of the River Somme with the support of tanks, these troops had quickly made spectacular advances. In the following weeks the enemy was remorselessly driven back on all fronts. Before the end of September, the Germans were back on the Hindenburg Line from where they had launched themselves on 21 March, just five months earlier. The conduct of the battle had been in marked contrast to earlier years, with commanders reinforcing troops who were advancing instead of those who were being checked.

Yet these astonishing gains were not achieved without heavy losses. The casualties in the last 100 days of the war reached the levels of the previous Somme and Ypres offensives of 1916 and 1917. With so many men still at the Front, it was inevitable that Westerham would take its share of killed and wounded. In the last days of September the fighting reached a crescendo as the Hindenburg position was assaulted and carried by the Allies. William Friend of the Canadian Army Service Corps was killed in action near Arras in this period of heavy fighting.

Private William Friend,
Canadian Army Service Corps

William Friend was born on 3 March 1880, the son of Alfred and Emma Friend of Moreton's Cottages, Westerham. After attending Hosey School, he emigrated to Canada where he worked as an engineer and fitter. By 1914 he had returned to England and was married, residing at Brocklehurst Street, New Cross, London. In 1916 he enlisted in the Canadian Army at Folkestone and served in France from 1917. His duties in the Army Service Corps involved transporting supplies and ammunition to the front line, often a hazardous task carried out under shellfire. It was while engaged in these duties he received wounds from which he died on 5 October 1918. William Friend is buried at Ficheux a few miles south of Arras. His widow, Florence, later lived at Manor Cottages, Westerham.

In late August 1918, Private Joe Cowell of Quebec Square, Westerham, was advancing with the 1st Royal West Kents near the town of Bapaume. On 29 August, his battalion was ordered forward as part of a general movement of the 5th Division. When his sergeant was killed, Joe took command of the platoon and led his men forward to the objective where he organised a spirited defence of the position. On being relieved, he also brought his men out through a shell-swept area. He was awarded the Distinguished Conduct Medal for his actions that day.

After the Hindenburg Line had been penetrated, the British Army found itself fighting in open country for the first time in four years. The Germans had no further prepared lines of defence on which to fall back, so the troops now advanced across land previously untouched by war. The enemy still mounted resolute rearguard actions but was never allowed to consolidate a position. Towards the end of October 1918, the British found themselves approaching the Belgian frontier and the area where the war began over four years earlier. Yet never at any time in the closing weeks of the war did the intensity of fighting slacken nor the level of casualties diminish.

* * *

The Machine Gun Corps had been born out of the need to give greater firepower to infantry units. At the beginning of the war, an infantry battalion was issued with two machine-guns but this number was rapidly increased as earlier battles demonstrated the value of massed volumes of fire. In October 1915, a dedicated unit was raised to specialise in these weapons. By 1916, a company of machine-gunners was attached to each infantry division, enabling continuous barriers, or barrages, of fire to be laid down for both defence and attack. The men who operated these weapons were, in the main, drawn from existing units and were sent on specialist courses held at corps training centres at Grantham and Bisley.

Private Charles Shepheard, 51st Battalion, Machine Gun Corps

In the final weeks of the war, the 51st Battalion Machine Gun Corps, part of the 51st Highland Division, was approaching the Belgian border near the town of Valenciennes. The machine-gunners were required to lay down a curtain of fire ahead of the attacking infantry, which would not only engage the enemy but also prevent the arrival of reinforcements.

On 24 October 1918, the Battalion supported an attack by the 153rd Infantry Brigade. Among the machine-gunners in action that day was Private Charles Shepheard of Westerham. Shepheard was born in 1896, the son of Thomas and Kate Shepheard of Chart Lane, Brasted, and at the outbreak of war he was living at Westerham Hill. After enlisting in the army, he initially served in the Royal Fusiliers.

Despite its successful outcome, the battle that was

fought between 24 and 26 October 1918 still produced a heavy toll of casualties. Charles Shepheard was among those missing at the end of the fighting and he is assumed to have been killed in action on the 26th. He has no known grave and is commemorated on the Vis-en-Artois Memorial, which lists those missing from the fighting of the last weeks of the war.

Popular mythology often considers that the First World War ended in a kind of stalemate through the exhaustion of the armies involved or in a final realisation of the war's futility. This is manifestly not true. Whatever the merits of the war, it ended as a result of the British Army, supported by Dominion and American forces, winning a stunning victory in the last months of 1918. Using all the hard-won experience of four years of fighting, from 8 August the British Army had conducted a lightning campaign, spearheading attacks with tanks and aircraft that repulsed the Germans on all fronts. From September the British were through the Hindenburg Line and in late October they were into Belgium where there was heavy fighting on the Sambre Canal and near Le Cateau, the scene of one the first actions in 1914. In common with most Great War battles, the casualty list of the last hundred days was enormous, running to some 300,000 in total. The scale of the fighting in the last months of the war inevitably caused further Westerham casualties. William Sales, (London Regiment) of Palin's Cottages was wounded in August, Harry Bradford, (Royal Lancaster Regiment), of Brewery Cottages, received gas poisoning and Thomas Nicholas (Royal West Kents), of High Street, was wounded in the chest. The final days of fighting also brought Westerham's penultimate fatality of the war.

Bombardier Charles Luttman, Royal Garrison Artillery

There is a unique sadness in the casualties of the last days of the war. For those who had already come through years of fighting, to be laid low in the final act is almost unbearably cruel. The poet Wilfred Owen was among those killed in the closing days of the war.

The death of Charles Luttman of French Street, Westerham, so close to the end of hostilities, has a heartbreaking poignancy. He had been a Reservist recalled to duty at the outbreak of war and had served in France with the Royal Horse Artillery from 1915. Prior to enlisting he had been a London policeman. Charles Luttman, who lived through nearly four years of fighting, died of wounds received in action while serving with an anti-aircraft battery during the general advance just north of Cambrai. He died on 29 October 1918 and was buried at Ramillies British Cemetery, Nord, France.

By the beginning of November 1918, both Austria and Turkey had capitulated and Germany had made the first overtures towards an armistice. On 7 November, negotiations began at Compiegne, France and on the 9th the German Kaiser abdicated. On 10 November the Germans accepted the Allies' terms.

At 11 a.m. on the following morning, the eleventh hour of the eleventh day of the eleventh month, the guns fell silent. By then the British were back in the vicinity of Mons where the first shots of the war had been fired in August 1914. Nearby, at St Symphorien, the first and the last British soldiers to die in the war lie within the same cemetery. On the day that victory was announced, Mrs Luttman of French Street, Westerham, received the news of the death of her husband, Charles. Even after four and a half years of tragedy there is no sadder commentary on the Great War.

Victory

At home, rumours of an Armistice had been circulating for some days. As Westerham returned to work after the weekend on Monday morning, 11 November 1918, it seemed that the impending news was more than people dared to hope. After nearly four and a half years of fighting, could the expectation actually become reality? The news that hostilities would end at 11 a.m. was finally confirmed by a telegraph message at the post office.

As the news spread rapidly through the town, people paused from their work to reflect on the enormity of what had happened. The continuous sounding of the brewery siren alerted men working in nearby woods and fields that the momentous news had arrived. Flags were soon appearing outside Mr Verrall's forge and across the walls of the brewery, bunting was also quickly strung from the upstairs windows of shops in the High Street. The bellringers hurriedly assembled at St Mary's and a victory peal soon rang out. At 6.30 p.m., a united service of thanksgiving was held at the parish church at which the Cadets, under Captain Cotton, paraded. The service was led by Canon Cooke in the absence of the Reverend Le Mesurier and the congregational minister, Reverend Dowswell, also participated. With the end of blackout restrictions, bonfires were lit on The Green and buildings were illuminated for the first time in years. Long-stored fireworks miraculously appeared to complete the festivities.

As the excitement subsided in the following days, people began to reflect on the cost of the war. For the many bereaved families in Westerham there would be no happy return to look forward to. The arrival of repatriated prisoners of war gave brief hopes to the families of soldiers listed as missing that perhaps their son or husband would return having been held, unrecorded, in captivity. Invariably these hopes would only fade in the coming weeks.

As the first peacetime Christmas in five years approached, the joy in many households would be matched by the sadness in others. Mrs Terry of Hosey still had no word of her husband Charles, missing at Arras since 1917. Mr and Mrs Knight of Madan Road still waited for news of their son Jack, missing at Cambrai a year before. The Batemans of Nursery Cottages were still seeking information on Charles, of whom no definite news had been received since March.

As the year of 1919 began there were still numerous reminders of the war and its aftermath. Many commodities, including coal, were still subject to rationing and the Westerham Territorials were still in India with no word of their imminent return. The National Service Committee workroom continued its output of garments for the many servicemen who were still overseas. Early in the New Year, George Hall of Madan Road and Archibald Ayres, whose parents lived in the High Street, both came home as repatriated prisoners of war, having been held in Germany since the March 1918 offensive. Also, in January 1919, Mrs Martin of 'The Larches', Madan Road, had the bittersweet task of attending the Maidstone barracks to receive her son's Military Medal, awarded for bravery in the field. Private Horace Martin had been killed in action before he could receive the award personally.

The beginning of 1919 saw no let up in the influenza epidemic that was sweeping Europe, and a number of deaths caused by the disease were recorded in the town. The pandemic was responsible for Westerham's last fatality of the Great War.

Private Robert English, 774th Company, Labour Corps

Robert English of Mill Street, born at Westerham in 1878, had been an employee of the Westerham brewery prior to enlisting in 1916. He served over two years in France in the Labour Corps who were employed in road and railway building, camp construction and the movement of stores, often in close proximity to the front line. After the Armistice, he returned to Westerham to administer the affairs of his parents who were both victims of the influenza epidemic. Early in 1919, he returned to Belgium where the Labour Corps were still fully employed in clearing the battlefields and removing stores and explosives. Shortly after his return, he also contracted the disease to which he succumbed on 8 February. Robert English is buried at Namur, Belgium. His daughter, Mrs Louisa Taylor, is still a Westerham resident.

Inevitably, as soon as the war ended, thoughts began to focus on the kind of memorial the town should provide as a fitting tribute to the men who had not come home. Various ideas and proposals were made: a swimming baths, a recreation ground and an institute were among the suggestions. A War Memorial Committee was formed, under the chairmanship of Mr E.C. Horton, to consider the options. The Committee contained many local luminaries including Charles Shawyer of the Parish Council, the Reverend Le Mesurier, Mrs Rooke, Dr Russell, Colonel Bonham Carter, Mr Bushell, Walter Rowe and Mr Forsey. Many of the proposals were aired at a public meeting, held in April 1919, which generated some heated debate. Most of the ambitious projects were ruled out on grounds of cost, although it was pointed out that Edenbridge was building a memorial hospital by combining with all the neighbouring villages. In the end, the argument seemed to be swayed by an impassioned letter from the vicar, printed in the *Westerham Herald*, which argued that whatever the town decided, some form of memorial should be placed at the parish church. This view seemed to be supported by many of the bereaved families. Eventually, a compromise was reached whereby a crucifix memorial would be erected in the churchyard and any surplus from the appeal fund would be donated to the new extension to the Sevenoaks Cottage Hospital.

As 1919 moved towards summer, many of the town's institutions resumed their peacetime activities. The National

Service Committee workroom finally closed its doors in March after four and a half years of prodigious output. The town band reformed under Albert Newton as more of its members were released from service. Walter Bennett, later to lead the band, came home from India at the end of March. The summer of 1919 also saw the reopening of the Swan Cinema.

On 6 July, on the conclusion of the peace treaty, a day of national celebration was held. A combined service of thanksgiving took place at the St Mary's, which was preceded by a parade and procession. Under the command of General Currie, the participants formed up at Squerryes before transiting the High Street to the parish church. The procession, led by the town band, included the returned servicemen, the Parish Council, special constables, the local firemen and other local volunteer organisations. Also, during the summer, a Comrades of the Great War association was formed – a forerunner of the British Legion.

It was not until nearly the end of the year that it was confirmed that the Territorials of the 1st/4th Battalion Royal West Kents were finally on their way home. After five years of foreign service, which included action on the North West Frontier in a war against Afghan tribesmen, the Battalion landed at Plymouth on 21 November. Following a rapturous welcome at Tonbridge, the Territorials were quickly dispersed. A planned welcome at the town station for the returning Westerham men was negated by the decision to release the men in small batches. However, the newly-returned servicemen were later entertained at the Crown Hotel with a welcome home dinner following an invitation, which read:

Your grateful fellow townsmen welcome you on your return home and have pleasure in inviting you to meet them at dinner on Thursday, 11th December, 1919 at the Crown Hotel at 6 p.m.

Nearly 80 'guests of the town', the majority of the returned Territorials, were entertained.

By 1920, most of the returned servicemen had begun to settle back into civilian life. Many had returned to their former employers like the Westerham Brewery and the local building traders. There were still many reminders of the war – a trophy in the form of a captured field gun was displayed on The Green, to the fascination of the town's schoolboys. A plaque was unveiled in the County and Westminster Bank, in memory of its former employee, Richard H. Blackaby, who was killed in 1916 (see p. 56).

For many of those who came home, shattered in mind and body, the war would never end. For those who had lost a son or a husband, the agony also continued.

On Sunday 15 August 1920, with due ceremony, the town's war memorial was unveiled and dedicated. The unveiling was performed by Lord Stanhope of Chevening (himself having lost an heir in the war) and the service was led by the Bishop of Rochester. Bereaved families were given prominence at the ceremony, which concluded with the sounding of The Last Post and the national anthem.

On 11 November 1920, there was finally an official recognition of the awful phenomenon of the missing of the Great War. On the second anniversary of the Armistice, and following a full state funeral, an Unknown Warrior was laid to rest in Westminster Abbey. 'Unknown' being symbolic of more than 300,000 men who died in the war having no known grave and 'Warrior' acknowledging that sailors and airmen as well as soldiers had all fought on the Western Front. The body of the unidentified soldier, selected at random from the battlefields of France and Flanders, had been brought across the Channel on a destroyer and conveyed by special train to Victoria Station where it was met by statesmen, princes and kings. The Unknown Warrior now lies among the great and powerful figures of history and symbolises Westerham men like Jack Knight, Albert Howard, Tom Quaife and Charles Bateman who simply disappeared into the holocaust of the Great War.

All too quickly, the war was subsumed by an even greater conflict. In September 1939, the men of Westerham once again marched off to war. This time, however, Britain was spared the casualties of a full Continental land war until the final year, for much of World War II Britain fought on its natural frontiers of the sea. This in no way diminishes the sacrifice of those who fought and died in the Second World War but, mercifully, our casualties were less than half those of the First and this is reflected on Westerham's war memorial. The Great War remains ingrained in the British psyche as epitomising all that is worst in war in terms of futility, waste, horror and sacrifice. Although this is understandable, the fact is that the Second World War was almost five times more destructive of human life than the First. There were atrocities in the Great War, there always are, but there was no Coventry, no Dresden, no Hiroshima and no Auschwitz. In 1918 our soldiers came home to a land that was still recognisable. The great battles of 1914–1918 were nearly all fought in open countryside. Visitors to the Great War battlefields can only wonder at the tranquillity that now prevails. Only the pristine war cemeteries that seem to abound at every corner bear witness to the tragedy that once unfolded.

In the 1970s, there was an upsurge of interest in the Great War. A spate of new books rekindled awareness and people began to enquire after grandfathers and great uncles who had served somewhere in France during the war of 1914–1918. Ease of transport also made the battlefields more accessible. It was surprising to learn that areas like the Somme and Ypres were no further from London than Manchester or Cardiff.

In 1979 the story of my uncle, Charles Albert Bateman, had been pieced together sufficiently to justify a journey that would hopefully retrace his footsteps through France. My father and I set off on a pilgrimage that took in towns like Cambrai, Albert, Pozieres and eventually ended on an open hillside a few miles south of St Quentin. It was there on 21 March 1918 that my father's elder brother was swept away in the onslaught of the last great German offensive. It was there that his story ended and the mystery began.

My father's family had pursued the quest for news of his fate relentlessly. Information was sought from officers of the battalion and from surviving comrades. All agreed that Sergeant Bateman was wounded on the day of the attack but, in the confusion of the retreat, nothing further could be confirmed. Eventually, all avenues of enquiry expired but never the hope that somehow he would turn up, safe and well. On that day in 1979, it seemed we were as close as we could ever be to knowing the fate of Charles Bateman.

Epilogue

So there the story has rested for over 80 years, until the recent research for this book uncovered a letter written in reply to the one of the many enquiries made by my father's family. The initial letter was sent to a Captain McDonald who was the senior surviving officer of the 7th Royal West Kents after 21 March 1918. It was forwarded to 2nd Lieutenant. E.A. Thomas who had commanded Sergeant Bateman's platoon. In August 1918, Thomas wrote:

> Your letter to Captain McDonald has been passed on to me for perusal. I am, however, sorry I cannot vouch any information about Sergeant Bateman other than he was going strong when I was rendered unable to carry on through wounds. I left my platoon in his charge at about 11 a.m. on 21 March, when we were fighting the Huns in the open. There is every chance, however, that he may be a prisoner of war. I do hope so.

This letter prompted a re-read of the regimental history, *The Queen's Own Royal West Kent Regiment 1914–1919*. A paragraph in the chapter detailing the 7th Battalion's actions on 21 March reads as follows (emphasis added):

> C [Company's] post at Le Vert Chasseur further to the right, which 2/Lt EA Thomas's platoon were holding, was attacked rather later. 2/Lt Thomas was wounded at the outset, *but the platoon sergeant took charge and put up a fine fight, holding the enemy at bay for some time; indeed it was only after he had been killed and the Lewis gun disabled that the post was finally rushed, only three survivors getting away.*

There at last, after nearly 90 years, was the information that always eluded my father's family. There at last is the news that would have brought some comfort and consolation to grieving parents. On 21 March 1918, Charles Bateman died a hero, taking charge of the position when his officer was disabled, and fighting on until overwhelmed.

Too late now for a family that had always sought this very detail. Too late for a mother who went to an early grave always believing that somehow her son would 'turn up'. Too late for my father who always spoke of a brother of whom 'we could never find out – we never knew', but now in memory, if nothing more, *Uncle Charlie comes home.*

Appendix 1

The Westerham Roll of Honour

Charles Adams 4th Bn. Royal West Kent Regt., New Street
Served in India. Received the India General Service Medal with bar
'Afghanistan: NW Frontier 1919'.

George Adams 4th Royal West Kent Regt., New Street

John Adams 15th London Regt. (Civil Service Rifles), New Street

Alfred Allen 4th Royal West Kent Regt., Mill Street
Invalided from Gallipoli. Later served in France where he was
wounded (shellshock). Discharged on 28 August 1917.

William Allen Royal West Kent Regt. & 20th Londons, Mill Street

George Walter Allen 1st Royal West Kent Regt., Mill Street
Killed in Action on 26 October 1917.

Arthur Anscombe Royal Navy, Vicarage Hill

Lionel Ashburner Captain, 4th Royal Fusiliers, 'Breaches'
Wounded at Mons, August 1914. Later served as Brigade Major of
32nd Inf. Div.

Hubert Askew Royal Flying Corps, Market Square

Robert Andrew Askew Army Service Corps, Market Square
Awarded the Military Medal for 'Bravery in the Field'. *London Gazette*
21 October 1918.

George Askew Army Service Corps, Market Square

Alec Askew Royal Flying Corps, Market Square

John Edward August Royal Sussex Regt., 'Oaklands'
Wounded in March 1918.

Joseph John Asser Lt. General, Commands and Staff., Darent Towers

Archibald Ayres 7th Royal West Kent Regt., High Street
Three times wounded. Prisoner of War from 21 March 1918. Lived at Thornton Heath, Surrey post war.

Frederick Baker Royal Field Artillery, Delegarde Farm
Wounded (gas poisoning) December 1917.

Horace Baker Army Service Corps
Served in Salonika.

Peter Barnett Royal West Kent Regt., Palin's Cottages
Served in the Royal West Kents receiving the Long Service Medal in 1927.

George William Barnett 2nd/4th Royal West Kent Regt., Palin's
  Cottages
Died of wounds in Egypt on 28 May 1917.

William Bashford Royal Navy, Park Cottages

Charles Albert Bateman 7th Royal West Kent Regt., Nursery Cottages
Killed in action on 21 March 1918.

Roy Roberts Bateman Bedfordshire Regt., Nursery Cottages

John A Bateman Royal Sussex Regt., Horns Hill
Wounded on the Somme in November 1916.

William J Bateman Royal Army Medical Corps., Horns Hill

John Beard 1st Royal West Kent Regt., Lodge Lane
Died of wounds on 20 July 1916.

Walter Elias Bennett 4th Royal West Kent Regt., Brewery Cottages
Served in India until March 1919. Later Westerham's Bandmaster.

Christopher John Benson Queen's (Royal West Surreys), High Street

Percy William Beresford Lt. Col., 2nd/3rd Bn. London Reg. 'The
  Laurels'
Awarded the Distinguished Service Order in 1917 for outstanding
leadership in action. Died of wounds on 26 October 1917.
Westerham's Curate and founder of the Cadets.

Arthur Baldry 2nd Lt., 14th Yorks and Lancs Regt., Pilgrim House
  School
Killed in Action on 4 December 1916.

William Jesse Bird 7th Royal West Kent Regt., Lodge Lane
Killed in Action on 14 February 1917.

Richard H Blackaby 1st East Kent Regt., (The Buffs)
Died of wounds on 18 September 1916. Formerly an employee of
Westminster Bank.

Sidney Thomas Blackman 3rd/4th Royal West Kents, London Road
Served in France from 1st June 1917.

Albert George Blake Royal West Kent Regt. & 13th Londons

George Blake 4th Royal West Kent Regt.
Served in India and received the India General Service Medal with
bar 'Afghanistan: NW Frontier 1919'.

David Blake 4th Royal West Kents & Kent Cyclist Battalion
Served in India. Received the India General Service Medal with bar
'Afghanistan: NW Frontier 1919'.

William Blissett Royal Horse Artillery, Quebec Square
Killed accidentally on 28 September 1914. Buried at Aisne, France.

Augustus James Bodman Army Service Corps.

Thomas Butler Bodman 7th Rifle Brigade, Greencroft, Farley
Killed in Action on 20 July 1915. Listed on the Menin Gate
Memorial, Ypres.

Albert Bone 2nd/12th London Regt., Hill Park
Died of wounds on 13 July 1917.

Herman Bonham Carter Colonel, Royal Engineers, 'Oak Lodge'

Philip H Bonham Carter Lt., Royal Navy, 'Oak Lodge'

Brian Hulbert Bonham Carter Lt., Indian Army, 'Oak Lodge'

Eric J Boreham Royal West Kent Regt., The Green
Served in the Middle East.

Harold J Boreham 2nd Bn. Welch Regiment, The Green
Enlisted in 1908 and served until 1919.

Thomas Bowles 7th Royal West Kent Regt., Hosey
Missing in Action after 21 March 1918. Later listed as a Prisoner of
War.

Walter Bowles Royal West Kent Regt.

Arthur Bond Royal Field Artillery, Delegarde Farm

Herbert George Brackley Flt. Lt., Royal Naval Air Service, High Street
Originally a Hosey School boy, later gaining a scholarship to
Sevenoaks School. Served with great distinction as an RNAS pilot,
gaining the DSO and DSC for carrying out bombing missions over
Belgium and the Western Front.

Samuel Bridgeland Army Service Corps, New Street

Harry J Bradford South Lancashire Regt., Brewery Cottages
Wounded in August 1917. Wounded (gas poisoning) in August 1918.

George Burgess 4th Royal West Kent & Royal Flying Corps, New
Street

Harold Burgess Royal West Kent Regt.

Herbert Burgess Royal West Kent Regt.

Edwin Herbert Catt Sub Lt., Royal Naval Division, 'Brunswick House'
Served in 'Howe' Battalion. Invalided from France in 1917.

Ernest Canfield Royal Naval Division, Squerryes Gardens
Served in 'Nelson' Battalion at Gallipoli and in France.

Arthur Canfield Army Service Corps, Squerryes Gardens

Ronald Canfield South Lancs. Regt., Squerryes Gardens

Edward Canfield Royal Engineers, Squerryes Gardens

Frank Clarke Australian Imperial Force, High Street

Edwin Clarke Royal Field Artillery

Albert Clarke Royal Naval Air Service

George Clarke Royal Flying Corps

Arthur Clemans Royal Garrison Artillery, Court Lodge Farm
Killed in Action on 17 November 1916. Battle of the Somme.

Ernest Cloke Royal Engineers, Madan Road

Frederick Walter Cull Royal Engineers, Duncans Yard

Frederick G Collins 4th Royal West Kent Regt.
Served in India and received the India General Service Medal with bar 'Afghanistan: NW Frontier, 1919'.

Alfred Charles Collins Royal Engineers

Arthur Cosgrove Royal Sussex Regt., Bloomfield Terrace
Wounded in April 1917.

Harry Cosgrove Royal Engineers, Bloomfield Terrace
Awarded the Military Medal for 'Bravery in the Field'. *London Gazette* 28 January 1918.

James Cosgrove Post Office Rifles, Bloomfield Terrace

Joseph Cosgrove Canadian Artillery, Bloomfield Terrace

Frank Cosgrove Bloomfield Terrace

William Cosgrove Royal Engineers, Bloomfield Terrace

Joseph Cowell 1st Royal West Kent Regt., Quebec Cottages
Awarded the Distinguished Conduct Medal for conspicuous gallantry
on 29 Aug.1918. Served in France from 23 June 1915. Twice
wounded: in November 1917 and September 1918.

George Cowell Royal West Kent Regt., Quebec Cottages

Douglas William James Cox 4th Royal West Kent Regt.
Served in India. Received the India General Service Medal with bar
'Afghanistan: NW Frontier, 1919'.

Arthur Cecil Currie CB, CMG. Brigadier General, Royal Garrison
  Artillery, 'Breaches'
Served in France from 2 March 1915.

John Cecil Currie Major, Royal Horse Artillery, 'Breaches'
Awarded the Military Cross for gallantry. Received the General Service
Medal with bar 'Iraq' and 'NW Persia'. This outstanding officer also
served through the Second World War, being awarded the DSO and
two bars. He was killed in Normandy, three weeks after D-Day. His
name is listed on the Westerham war memorial for World War II.

Percy Darlington Royal Welsh Fusiliers, 'Well House'
Severely wounded in April 1918.

Allen Grant Douglas Captain, 14th Londons (London Scottish),
  Farley House
Awarded the Military Cross for conspicuous gallantry and devotion
to duty during the Battle of Arras. Killed in Action at Cambrai on 30
November 1917.

Francis William Radford Douglas Lt., Royal Field Artillery, Farley House

Andrew Douglas Downs 1st London Regt. (Royal Fusiliers), Valence. Served at Gallipoli. Severely wounded on 15th September 1916.

David Downs Cameron Highlanders & Royal Flying Corps, Valence

John T Downs 7th London Regt. & Machine Gun Corps, Valence

Henry R Drapper 4th Royal West Kents & South Staffs, Mill Street

Edward J Drapper Royal Army Medical Corps, Mill Street

George Dale Royal Sussex Regt., Dunsdale Lodge

George William Dale Royal Naval Air Service

Albert Dyer Royal Army Medical Corps

John Edmunds Lt., 1st Surrey Rifles (21st Londons), 'The Stores'
Awarded the Military Cross. Wounded on 25 August 1918.

Harry English 4th Royal West Kents Regt. Mill Street
Served in India

Robert English Labour Corps, Mill Street
Died of influenza on 8 February 1919.

Albert Walter Fennell East Surrey Regt., Force Green
Twice wounded in the war, no doubt contributing to his early death, aged 21, in 1919. Buried in St Mary's churchyard and marked by a War Graves headstone.

George Harry Fennell 8th Royal West Kent Regt., Force Green
Killed in Action on 21 November 1916.

Harry John Stanley Fenton Army Service Corps
Mobilised in 1914, fought at Mons. Formerly worked at Evenden's Garage.

Arthur Frederick Finch Royal Garrison Artillery, Bellvue Terrace, New Street

Charles James Fisk 10th Australian Infantry. Coorabie, South Australia, late of High Street.
Served at Gallipoli, 1915. Killed in Action in France on 23 August 1916.

Frederick Ford 18th Hussars, 'The King's Arms'
Enlisted 1 September 1906. Discharged 19 March 1919.

Christopher Ford Royal Engineers, The Green

Herbert R Ford East Surrey Regt., The Green

Hugh Alfred Fuller Honourable Artillery Company, High Street

Arthur George Fuller Royal West Kent Regt., The Paddock (post war)

Cyril Fuller Bedfordshire Regt.

William Friend Canadian Army Service Corps, Manor Cottages
Died of wounds on 5 October 1918.

John Charles Friend Royal Flying Corps

Frederick Gallop 6th Royal West Kent Regt., Madan Road
Wounded on the Somme in 1916. Discharged in 1917.

George Thomas Gardiner Royal Navy, Madan Road
Served in HMS *Beagle*.

Harry Gardiner 4th Royal West Kent Regt., South Bank
Served in India. Received the India General Service Medal with bar 'Afghanistan: NW Frontier, 1919'.

William Gibbs Bedfordshire Regt.

Douglas W Genge Honourable Artillery Company, Market Square
Enlisted 1912. Discharged 31 January 1917.

William Stanley Gooding Royal Engineers, South Bank
Killed in Action on 31 May 1918.

Daniel Gramson 4th Royal West Kent Regt., Mill Street
Subsequently received a commission into the Indian Army.

John Henry Gramson Royal West Kent Regt.

Charles Graddon Captain, 13th Kings Royal Rifle Corps.
Served in France from 30 July 1915.

James Gordon Hamilton Greig 2nd Lt., 6th Bn. East Kent Regt., 'The
  Mount'
Died of wounds on 13 August 1915.

Edgar Gurr 4th Royal West Kents & Machine Gun Corps, South Bank
Served in France from 1 June 1915.

Frederick Gurr Royal West Kents & Notts and Derby Regt., South
  Bank

Edward Martin Guy OBE Captain, Northumberland Hussars,
  'Pilgrims'

George Hall 1st Bn. Wiltshire Regt., Madan Road
Prisoner of War from 12 April 1918.

Geoffrey Hamlin 13th London Regiment.

Edwin Stephen Hammond Royal Navy

Harold Hatcher South Lancashire Regt., New Streeet
Prisoner of war from 7 March 1918.

William Augustus Hayward Royal Sussex Regt. & Labour Corps,
  Moreton's Cottages
Served at Mons. Twice wounded. Former Westerham postman.

George Alfred Hider Grenadier Guards, 'Horsemans Cottage'
Served in France from Aug 1914 to May 1915. Died at Westerham on
8 May 1918.

Alfred John Hoath Army Service Corps, South Bank

Frederick Hoath Royal Marines, South Bank
Served at Jutland, May 1916, on HMS *Phaeton*, and Zeebrugge Raid, April 1918, where he received a Mention in Despatches.

Harry Hoath 4th Royal West Kent Regt., High Street
Served in India. Received the India General Service Medal with bar 'Afghanistan NW Frontier 1919'.

Henry Russell Hoath 4th Royal West Kents & 20th London Regt., South Bank
Wounded on 1 October 1916 during the Battle of the Somme.

William Hoath 4th Royal West Kent Regt., High Street
Invalided from India in 1917.

Harold Victor Hobbis 8th Bn. Bedfordshire Regt., Madan Road

Percy Hobbis Royal Flying Corps

Charles William Hooker 4th Royal West Kent Regt., Westbury Terrace
Company Sergeant Major with local Territorials, ('H' Coy.) Leader of Westerham firemen.

Ernest Hooker 4th Royal West Kents & Royal Welsh Fusiliers, High Street
Served at Gallipoli.

Thomas Hooker Army Service Corps

William Hollands Royal West Kent Regt., Madan Road

Henry Haggard Brigadier General., 32nd Brigade & General Staff, 'Breaches'

Sydney Harrison DCM
Astute readers may have noticed that one man, listed on the Westerham memorial, is not mentioned in the preceding text. Despite extensive research, it has proved impossible to identify the Westerham Sydney Harrison from around 20 men of that name who

died in WWI. Not even the Distinguished Conduct Medal rolls have been helpful in this respect. No doubt these pages will elicit an immediate response but for the moment the file on Sydney Harrison remains open.

George Heath Royal Navy, Railway Terrace
Served over 25 years. Survivor of the sinking of HMS *Natal*.

Harold Howard Royal West Kents & Kings Royal Rifle Corps, Springfield Cottages

Herbert Howard Royal West Kents & Northants. Regt., Springfield Cottages
Wounded on 12 December 1917.

Albert Charles Howard Queens Royal West Surreys, Springfield Cottages
Killed in Action on 8 August 1918.

Ambrose Langley Hunt Master, 'SS *Burrsfield*', 'Old Hill House'
Killed in the sinking of the '*Burrsfield*' on 5 October 1915.

James Hunt Royal Engineers, Railway Terrace
Prisoner of War from November 1917.

Henry Igglesden Army Service Corps, London Road

James Alfred Pigou Inglis Lt. Royal Engineers, 'The Nest', French Street
Killed in Action at the Battle of Loos on 25 September 1915.

Frank James Jarrett Royal Engineers, London Road

James T Jarrett Army Ordnance Corps, Vicarage Hill

Edward F Jarrett Royal Sussex Regt., Vicarage Hill

William Henry Jarrett Middlesex Regt., Vicarage Hill

Harry Frederick Jarrett Lancashire Fusiliers, Vicarage Hill
Prisoner of War from August 1916.

Henry Jealous West Kent Yeomanry
Served at Gallipoli from 7 October 1915.

John Jupp 4th Royal West Kent Regt. & East Kent Regt., London Road
Served in India and Mesopotamia.

Charles Jupp West Yorkshire Regt., London Road
Wounded in 1918. (Son of John Jupp)

Henry George Jupp Royal Artillery
Served in France from 16 August 1914.

Arthur Jenner 8th Bn. Queens Royal West Surreys, Valence
Awarded the Military Medal for 'Bravery in the Field'. *London Gazette* 17 June 1919.

Robert Jenner Royal Navy, Valence

William Robert Keeley Royal Fusiliers & Royal Sussex Regt., Madan Road
Wounded (gas poisoning) in May 1917.

Ernest J Kimber West Kent Yeomanry & 8th Royal West Kents, Vicarage Hill
Enlisted 14 November 1914. Discharged 22 December 1917.

Arthur Kimber Army Service Corps.
Served in East Africa.

Sydney Charles King 10th Bn. Queen's Royal West Surreys, New Street
Killed in action in Italy, 7 January 1918.

James Walter (Jack) Knight 3rd Bn. Grenadier Guards, Madan Road
Killed in action at Cambrai on 27 November 1917.

John Christopher Lander 1st London Scottish, Betsom's Farm
Killed in action at Cambrai on 24 November 1917.

Arthur Horace Lang 2nd Lt., Grenadier Guards attd. Scots Guards, 'Breaches'
Killed in action at Cuinchy, France on 25 January 1915.

Archibald Edward Langridge Royal Navy, 'Stakes House'
Killed in the Chatham air raid on 3 September 1917.

William Henry Langridge Royal Navy HMS *Princess Royal*

Sidney Lambert 1st Royal West Kent Regt., Former Squerryes
gamekeeper
Severely wounded in July 1916. Discharged 26 July 1917.

Norrie Alfred Leney 22nd Royal Fusiliers, New Street
Killed in action at Arras on 29 April 1917.

Frederick Leppard East Surrey Regt., Lodge Lane
Formerly the manager of the 'International Stores'. Wounded in 1917.

Charles Henry Leftley Royal West Kents & Norfolk Regt.
Served in France from 1 June 1915.

Thomas Levett Queen's Royal West Surrey Regt.

Charles W Lockyer 4th Royal West Kent Regt., French Street
Served five years in India. Received the India General Service Medal
with bar 'Afghanistan: NW Frontier, 1919'.

Herbert R Lockyer 4th Royal West Kent Regt., French Street
Served five years in India. Received the India General Service Medal
with bar 'Afghanistan: NW Frontier, 1919'.

Obediah Lockyer 4th Royal West Kent Regt., French Street

George Libbell 4th Royal West Kent Regt.
Served in India. Received the India General Service Medal with bar
'Afghanistan: NW Frontier, 1919'.

Frederick Lurcook West Kent Yeomanry & Middx. Regt., Former
Westerham postman

Charles Luttman Royal Garrison Artillery, French Street
Died of wounds on 29 October 1918.

Alfred Ernest Marks Royal Naval Air Service

Henry Martin Royal Navy, HMS *Glowworm*, Railway Terrace

William Charles Martin Royal West Kent Regt., Railway Terrace
Served in France from June 1916. Wounded in July 1916. Later
Prisoner of War.

Harry Martin Royal West Kent Regt., Madan Road
Died at Westerham on 28 August 1917.

Chas. Henry Horace Martin 6th Bn. Royal West Kent Regt., Madan
    Road
Son of Harry Martin. Awarded the Military Medal for 'Bravery in the
Field'. Killed in action on 30 June 1918.

Albert Edward Moseley Royal Engineers

Thomas Henry Martle 4th Royal West Kent Regt., Stratton Terrace
Westerham's Territorials Instructor. Invalided from Gallipoli in 1915.

Ernest Matthews Durham Light Infantry, Nursery Cottages
Served in the Salonika campaign.

Andrew Gordon Maynard Army Ordnance Corps

Herbert H Medhurst Middlesex Regt. & Royal Fusiliers, The Green
    (post war)
Wounded on the Somme in 1916. Records show HH Medhurst enlisted
9 December 1915 and was discharged (wounds) 31 March 1919.

Harry A Miles Army Service Corps, 'Southview'
Served in France from 24 November 1914.

John Miles Tank Corps, Madan Road

William Miles Royal Engineers, London Road
Wounded on the Somme in July 1916.

George Miles Army Service Corps

Arthur Charles Mills Royal Garrison Artillery, The Green
Served in France from 31 August 1915. Wounded in September 1917.

George Edward Munday Middlesex Regt., Madan Road
Wounded at Mons in August 1914 and at Hill 60 in May 1915.

John Newman 4th Royal West Kent Regt., Palin's Cottages
Served in India. Received the India General Service Medal with bar
'Afghanistan: NW Frontier, 1919'.

William Newman Royal West Kent Regt., London Road
Served in India. Received the India General Service Medal with bar
'Afghanistan: NW Frontier, 1919'.

Alfred Nicholas West Yorkshire Regt., High Street

Thomas C Nicholas Royal West Kent Regt., High Street
Wounded in August 1918.

Albert E Newton 1st Royal West Kent Regt., The Green
Served in France from 7 December 1914. Discharged through sickness
on 23 June 1915. Westerham's band master.

Edward A Newton 4th Royal West Kent Regt., The Green
Served in India. Received the India General Service Medal with bar
'Afghanistan: NW Frontier, 1919'.

Frank Leslie Newton Lt., 11th Hampshire Regt., 'Bincleaves'
Received wounds to the right leg on 30 March 1918. Discharged on
28 February 1919.

Leonard Newton Lt., Royal Navy. HMS *Orion*.

Herbert Steer Outrim The Buffs (East Kent Regt), Lodge Lane
Enlisted 10 December 1915. Wounded May 1917. Discharged 2
February 1918.

Ernest James Outrim Army Service Corps, Lodge Lane

Arthur Henry Outrim Royal Garrison Artillery, Lodge Lane

Edward John Outrim Middlesex Regt., Lodge Lane

Stanley Old 9th Bn. Middlesex Regt.
Served in India.

Frederick Charles Paige 4th Royal West Kent Regt., Mill Street
Served in India. Received the India General Service Medal with bar 'Afghanistan: NW Frontier, 1919'.

Alec John Parkhurst Royal Navy, Market Square
Lost in the sinking of HMS *Hampshire* on 5 June 1916.

John Thomas Parkins 8th Hussars & Royal Field Artillery
Awarded the Military Medal for 'Bravery in the Field'. *London Gazette* 13 March 1919.

Richard Payne Army Service Corps
Wounded October 1917.

Ian Campbell Penney Captain, 13th Bn. Royal Scots, 'The Knoll'
Killed in action at the Battle of Loos on 26 September 1915.

Colin Moncrieff Penney Lt., Kings Royal Rifle Corps 'The Knoll'
Prisoner of War from 30 November 1917.

Keith Brodie Penney 2nd Lt., West Yorks Regt., 'The Knoll'

John William Penfold 13th Canadian Infantry, Railway Terrace
Died at Westerham on 18 February 1915.

Frederick Charles Penfold Royal West Kent Regt.

Harold Denis Pennicard Army Veterinary Corps, Farley
Died in the influenza epidemic at Dieppe, France on 11 June 1918.

Herbert Peters 4th Royal West Kents, High Street
Served in India. Received the India General Service Medal with bar 'Afghanistan: NW Frontier, 1919'.

Dudley Frank Peters Royal Naval Volunteer Reserve

Chris Morris George Pickett 27th Australian Infantry, Railway Terrace
Served at Gallipoli and in France. Enlisted at Coorabie, South Australia. Awarded the Military Medal for 'Bravery in the Field'. *London Gazette* 20 Aug 1919.

William Edward Pickett Royal West Kent Regt., Mill Street
Awarded the Croix de Guerre.

Jesse Pickett Royal West Kent Regt., Railway Terrace

Charles Phillips Royal Warwickshire Regt., Springfield Cottages
Severely wounded 26 August 1917 resulting in a leg amputation.

Albert Phillips 4th Royal West Kents & Post Office Rifles, Rysted
Lane
Wounded in 1918. Later served in Labour Corps.

Albert Pope 4th Royal West Kent Regt., French Street

Wallace Pritchard Lt., Australian Infantry, 'Aberdeen House'
Three times wounded (on 3 May 1918 losing part of his left hand).

Ralph Pritchard Royal Field Artillery

Reginald M Pyke Royal Flying Corps

Tom Quaife 6th Bn. The Buffs (East Kent Regt.), Mill Street
Killed in action at the Battle of Arras on 1 May 1917.

Alfred Richards Army Service Corps, 'George and Dragon' Inn

George Richardson Royal Navy

Frederick Ring Royal Flying Corps, New Street

Humphrey I Robinson Lieutenant, Royal West Kent Regt.

James Frederick Martyn Robinson Captain, East Yorks Yeomanry,
Betsom's Hill
Awarded the Military Cross for gallantry. *London Gazette* 27 October
1917.

Charles Mills Rose Army Ordnance Corps, Old Vicarage Cottage
Served in France from 15 August 1914. Awarded the Meritorious
Service Medal. *London Gazette* 4 June 1917.

Leslie Rowe 4th Royal West Kent Regt. Squerryes Gardens
Served in India.

Walter Henry Rowe 4th Royal West Kent Regt., Squerryes Garden
Commissioned into the Indian Army on 4 November 1917.

Frank Thomas Russell 4th Royal West Kent Regt., London Road
Served in India.

William Stephen Sales Royal West Kents, Royal Fusiliers, Middx Regt.
& London Regt., Vicarage Hill
Wounded in April 1917 and in August 1918.

Horace Sales Army Service Corps, Vicarage Hill
Served in France from 12 August 1914.

Montague W Sayers Royal West Kent Regt., London Road
Wounded in 1916. Prisoner of War from 21 March 1918.

Frederick Robert Sayers Royal Naval Division, London Road
Served in 'Hawke' Battalion at Gallipoli and in France.

Arthur Saxby Royal Flying Corps, Madan Road

Nathan George Salmon Australian Field Artillery, Grange Cottages
Killed in action at Gallipoli on 25 August 1915.

Ernest Salmon West Kent Yeomanry & East Kent Regt., Grange
Cottages
Wounded at Gallipoli. Survivor of the sinking of Troopship '*Ivernia*'
on 1 January 1917. Later commissioned into the RAF.

Frederick Salmon West Kent Yeomanry & East Kent Regt., Grange
Cottages
Received a commission into the Indian Army in 1918.

Arthur Salmon East Kent Regt. 'The Buffs', Grange Cottages
Wounded in April 1917.

Arthur Charles Sharp Army Service Corps

Jack Shawyer Army Service Corps, Market Square

Charles W Shearing 9th London Regt., South Bank

George Alfred Douglas Shearing Royal Field Artillery, South Bank
Killed in action at the Battle of the Somme on 14 August 1916.

William Singleton Royal Marines, New Street
Served at Dunkirk in 1914. Wounded at Gallipoli in 1915. Present at
the Battle of Jutland.

Albert Singleton Royal Navy, New Street

Henry Singleton Royal Field Artillery, New Street
Killed in Action on 27 October 1917.

Charles Shepheard Royal Fusiliers & Machine Gun Corps, Westerham
  Hill
Killed in Action on 26 October 1918.

Edward Chas. Smith 7th Royal West Kent Regt., Lodge Lane
Killed in Action on 27 May 1917.

Joseph Smith 4th Royal West Kent Regt., French Street
Served in India. Received the India General Service Medal with bar
'Afghanistan: NW Frontier, 1919'.

Frederick Nathan Smith West Kent Yeomanry & East Kent Regt.
Served at Gallipoli from 24 September 1915.

Alfred Smith 2nd/4th Royal West Kents
Served at Gallipoli.

Frederick Shergold Royal Army Medical Corps, 'Rooks Nest'

Richard Charles Shergold Royal West Kent Regt., 'Rooks Nest'
Wounded (Gas poisoning) 1917. Discharged in 1918.

Henry Thos. Shergold Royal Berkshire Regt., 'Rooks Nest'
Wounded in 1917.

Edwin Shergold Royal Army Medical Corps, 'Rooks Nest'

147

George Simmons 2nd Lt., 8th Bn. East Surrey Regt., 'The Hollies'
Wounded by artillery fire on 10 August 1917.

George AS Selby 4th Royal West Kent Regt., Madan Road
Served in India. Received the India General Service Medal with bar
'Afghanistan: NW Frontier, 1919'.

Frederick HS Selby Royal West Kents & 13th London Regt., Madan
  Road
Wounded in March 1917.

Clifford Selby Essex Regiment., Madan Road
Wounded (Gas poisoning) in March 1918.

Arthur J Selby Honourable Artillery Company, Madan Road

George Cotgrave Spillar Royal Navy. HMS *Lord Nelson*
Died in the influenza epidemic in March 1919.

Alfred George Steer West Kent Yeomanry, Madan Road

Robert Stone 4th Royal West Kent Regt., New Street
Served in India. Received the India General Service Medal with bar
'Afghanistan: NW Frontier, 1919'.

George Stroner 8th Royal West Kent Regt., French Street
Served in France from 1915. Discharged (wounds) in December 1917.

Albert Harold Octavius Streatfeild Lt., Royal Sussex Regiment,
  Crockham Street
Served in France from 15 June 1915.

Granville Edward Stewart Streatfeild Major, Royal Engineers, Hosey
Awarded the Distinguished Service Order. *London Gazette* 4 June
1917.

Arthur Streatfield 4th Royal West Kent Regt., Mill Cottages
Invalided from India in 1917.

Benjamin Streatfield Royal Field Artillery

Arthur George Stephens Canadians, Vicarage Hill

George Stevens 4th Royal West Kent Regt.
Served in India. Received the India General Service Medal with bar 'Afghanistan: NW Frontier, 1919'.

Charles Richard Sullivan Hospital Ship '*Rewa*', High Street
Survived the sinking of the '*Rewa*', torpedoed in the Bristol Channel on 4 January 1918.

Charles Lawrence Taylor 4th Royal West Kent Regt., High Street
Served in India. Received the India General Service Medal with bar 'Afghanistan: NW Frontier, 1919'.

Alfred G Taylor 2nd/4th Royal West Kent Regt., Valence

Charles Terry 17th Bn. Middlesex Regt., Hosey Avenue
Killed in action on 28 April 1917.

John Archibald Terry Royal West Kents & Royal Fusiliers, Church Alley
Wounded at Arras on 28 April 1917.

Percy Thorneycroft Royal Fusiliers, Church Alley
Prisoner of War from March 1918.

Arthur R Thorpe Leicestershire Regiment, Former Hosey School teacher.
Invalided from France in 1918.

Arthur Bell Townsend 4th Royal West Kent Regt., High Street
Served in India. Received the India General Service medal with bar 'Afghanistan: NW Frontier, 1919'.

Frank John Townsend Army Service Corps, High Street

Albert Townsend Royal Navy, High Street

James Utting Army Service Corps, Stratton Terrace
Served in France from 23 August 1914 and later in the RAF.

Arthur Edward Vaus Royal Engineers, London Road

Cyril Vaus Royal Engineers, New Street

Raymond Vivian Vaus Royal West Kent Regt., High Street

Harold Verrall Honourable Artillery Company, The Forge, High
Street
Invalided in July 1917.

William Wallace Royal Flying Corps.

Edmund A Waterhouse 4th Royal West Kent Regt.

James Waterhouse Army Service Corps, Madan Road

Sidney Watts Royal Navy. HMS *Nimrod*, Bloomfield Terrace

Albert Watts Australian Infantry, Bloomfield Terrace
Wounded at Messines in 1917 (Gas poisoning).

Henry Watts Royal Navy, Bloomfield Terrace

Charles T Ward 4th Royal West Kent Regt.
Received the General Service Medal for S Persia.

John Roberts O'Brien Warde Major, Royal Artillery, Squerryes Court
Served in France from 19 June 1917.

Charles Norman Watney Colonel, 4th Royal West Kent Regt.,
Valence
Commanded the 1st/4th Battalion in India.

Gerrard Norman Watney Captain. Royal West Kents and KOYLI
Served in France from 4 May 1916.

Richard W Wade Royal Sussex Regiment, Brewery Cottages
Died at Newhaven on 28 November 1916. Buried at Westerham.

Wallace Wade Royal Navy, Brewery Cottages

Walter Wakeford Royal Lancaster Regiment, High Street
Served in France from 18 August 1915. Severely wounded at Messines, June 1917.

Walter Ruggles Webb 2nd Grenadier Guards, Duncan's Yard
Fought at Mons in 1914. Severely wounded and later invalided and discharged.

William Arthur Weller 1st Royal West Kent Regt., High Street
Killed in Action on 10 February 1917.

Samuel Webster Royal West Kent Regt.

William Thomas Wells London Regiment, Croydon Road
Wounded in October 1917.

James Wells Army Service Corps

Robert Wells Royal West Kent Regt.
Wounded in April 1917.

Henry Wheeler Royal West Kent Regt.
Served in France from 22 April 1916.

Alfred Thomas White 2nd/4th Royal West Kents, 'Greencroft'

Henry Whitebread Army Service Corps, Church Alley

John Whitebread Royal Garrison Artillery, Church Alley
Killed in action on 28 March 1918.

Albert Whiting 4th Royal West Kents & Royal Engineers, Quebec Square

Frederick Whiting 4th Royal West Kent Regt., Madan Road
Served in India. Received the India General Service Medal with bar 'Afghanistan: NW Frontier, 1919'.

Walter Whiting 4th Royal West Kent Regt., Quebec Square

151

George Whiting Durham Light Infantry

George E Whitmore 4th Royal West Kents & South Staffs Regt., 'Crown Hotel'

Hubert George Willson Suffolk Yeomanry

Edgar Gordon Wise Royal Garrison Artillery, Madan Road

Alfred Ernest Wood 9th Bn. Norfolk Regiment, French Street
Killed in action on 15 April 1918.

Horace Frank Wood 8th Royal West Kent Regt., French Street
Wounded at Loos in 1915 and again at Arras in April 1917.

Albert Henry Wood Queen's Westminster Rifles, French Street
Wounded in 1917.

Percy Frederick Wood 4th Royal West Kent Regt., French Street
Served in India. Received the India General Service Medal with bar 'Afghanistan: NW Frontier, 1919'.

Charles Wood Royal Fusiliers, French Street

William George Wood Army Service Corps, Quebec Cottages

Albert William Wood Royal West Kent Regt., Forge Cottage
Invalided from Gallipoli. Wounded in France on 19 April 1917.

George Wood Royal West Kent Regt., Railway Terrace
Prisoner of war on 24 March 1918.

Ernest Wood 2nd/7th Notts and Derby Regt., Lodge Lane
Killed in action on 27 September 1917.

William Thomas Williams Royal West Kent Regt.

William Frederick Woolgar Royal West Kents & Kent Cyclist Battalion.
Served in India. Received the India General Service Medal with bar 'Afghanistan: NW Frontier, 1919'.

George Obed Wood Royal Navy, Park Cottages
Lost on HMS *Turbulent* at the Battle of Jutland on 31 May 1916.

Edward Wood 4th Royal West Kent Regt., High Street
Served in India. Received the India General Service Medal with bar
'Afghanistan: NW Frontier, 1919'.

John Yorkston 2nd Bn. Leicestershire Regt., Madan Road
Enlisted in 1910. Served in France from 12 October 1914. Discharged
through wounds and sickness in 1919.

Archibald Harry Yorkston Royal Naval Air Service, Madan Road

Frederick Yorkston Rifle Brigade, Madan Road
Served in France from 30 May 1915. Wounded on the Somme on 7
July 1916. Wounded and taken Prisoner of War on 27 May 1918.

Alec Gibson Yorkston Durham Light Infantry, Madan Road

Leslie N Yorkston 4th Royal West Kent Regt., Madan Road
Served in India. Received the India General Service Medal with bar
'Afghanistan: NW Frontier, 1919'.

Appendix 2

Westerham Honours and Awards

Distinguished Service Order

Percy William Beresford 2nd/3rd London Regt., 'The Laurels'
At Bullecourt, France on 15 May, 1917 the 2nd/3rd Londons, commanded by Col. Beresford, were attacked by waves of enemy infantry who partially overran the battalion on their right. The Londons beat off these attacks and gave support to the flanking unit enabling them to regain their positions. The Londons suffered over 200 casualties in the action.

London Gazette 18.7.1917

Herbert George Brackley Royal Naval Air Service, (formerly) High Street
In recognition of his services on 14 April 1917 when he carried out a successful raid on Bruges harbour. The raid was carried with persistence and determination despite difficult conditions. He also dropped bombs on the Ostend seaplane base on the night of 3rd/4th May 1917, making two raids.

London Gazette 22.6.1917

Granville Edward Stewart Streatfeild Royal Engineers, Hosey

London Gazette 4.6.1917

Distinguished Service Cross

Herbert George Brackley Royal Naval Air Service, (formerly) High Street
Awarded for conspicuous good work as the pilot of a bombing aircraft. He carried out twelve raids from 1 June 1916 mostly by night, returning on one occasion with forty holes in his aircraft.

London Gazette 12.5.1917

Military Cross

John Cecil Currie Royal Horse Artillery, 'Breaches', Vicarage Hill

London Gazette 3.6.1918

Allen Grant Douglas 14th London Regt. (London Scottish), Farley
At the Battle of Arras in April 1917 he performed the duties of Adjutant with great energy and efficiency. He went forward and, reorganising the Companies, formed a bombing attack which cleared the enemy out of the trenches. This task was carried out under continuous shell fire.

London Gazette 18.7.1917

John Edmunds 21st London Regt. (1st Surrey Rifles), 'The Stores'
During the retreat following the German spring offensive of 1918, he remained in the front line with another officer and a few men for four hours after the position had been evacuated. This task was carried out with great ability and, at the appointed time, he withdrew without a casualty and without the enemy suspecting that the line had been evacuated.

London Gazette 18.7.1918

J F Martyn Robinson East Yorkshire Yeomanry, Betsom's Hill
When in command of a patrol within 200 yards of the enemy, one man had his horse shot under him. Captain Martyn Robinson rode up and carried the man to safety while still under enemy fire.

London Gazette 27.10.1917

Distinguished Conduct Medal

Joseph Cowell 1st Bn. Royal West Kent Regt., Quebec Cottages
Near Bapaume, France on 29th August 1918, Pte Cowell was advancing with his platoon. When the platoon sergeant became a casualty, Joe Cowell took command and led his men forward under complete control. He established contact with flanking units and consolidated the new position. On being relieved on the 30th, he brought his men out through a shell swept area.

London Gazette 5.12.1918

(Joe Cowell was presented with his medal during the Peace Day celebrations of July 1919 at a ceremony in the Market Square in front of a small parade of returned serviceman. The presentation was made by Brigadier General Currie of 'Breaches', Vicarage Hill.)

Military Medal

Robert Andrew Askew Army Service Corps, Market Square
Awarded for 'Bravery in the Field'
London Gazette 21.10.1918

Harry Cosgrove Royal Engineers, Bloomfield Terrace
Awarded for 'Bravery in the Field'
London Gazette 28.1.1918

John Thomas Parkins Royal Field Artillery
Awarded For 'Bravery in the Field'
London Gazette 13.3.1919

Charles Henry Horace Martin 6th Royal West Kent Regt., Madan Road
Awarded For 'Bravery in the Field'
London Gazette 17.9.1917

Chris. Morris George Pickett Australian Infantry, Railway Terrace
Awarded for 'Bravery in the Field'
London Gazette 20.8.1919

Arthur Edward Jenner 7th Queen's (Royal West Surreys), Valence
Awarded for 'Bravery in the Field'
London Gazette 17.6.1919

Meritorious Service Medal

Charles E Rose Army Ordnance Corps, Old Vicarage Cottage
London Gazette 4.6.1917

Mention in Despatches

Frederick Hoath Royal Marines, South Bank
MID for the famous Zeebrugge Raid on St Georges Day, 1918. Fred Hoath was part of the Royal Marine contingent on the assault ship '*Iris*'.

Henry Igglesden Army Service Corps, London Road

Charles M Rose Army Ordnance Corps, Old Vicarage Cottage

Edward Newton 1st/4th Royal West Kent Regt., The Green
Edward Wood 1st/4th Royal West Kent Regt., High Street
Percy William Wood 1st/4th Royal West Kent Regt., French Street

The three above named Westerham men were recommended for a Mention in Despatches for the action at Spin Maldak on the Northwest Frontier during the Afghan War, May 1919. All three men were bandsmen who acted as stretcher bearers during the action.

Bibliography

Atkinson, CT, *The Queen's Own Royal West Kent Regiment 1914–1919*, Simpkin, 1924

Berkeley, Reginald, MC, *The History of the Rifle Brigade in the War of 1914–1918, Volume 1*, The Rifle Brigade Club, 1927

Coombs, REB, *Before Endeavours Fade*, After The Battle, 1976

Farrar-Hockley, AH, *The Somme*, Batsford, 1964

Gallimore, Kathy, *Westerham: A Kiwi Returns to Her Nest*, Book Guild, 2003

Gliddon, Gerald, *The Battle of the Somme: A Topographical History*, Sutton Publishing, 1994

Headlam, Cuthbert, DSO, *The Guards Division in the Great War*, John Murray, 1924

Keegan, John, *The First World War*, Hutchinson, 1998

Kemp, Paul, *The Admiralty Regrets: British Warship Losses in the 20th Century*, Sutton Publishing, 1999

Lindsay, JH, Lt Col, *The London Scottish in the Great War*, Regimental Headquarters, 1926

Middlebrook, Martin, *The First Day on the Somme*, Allen Lane, The Penguin Press, 1971

Molony, CV, *Invicta: With the 1st Bn. R W Kent Regt. in the Great War*, Nisbet, 1923

Moody, RSH, *Historical Records of the Buffs, East Kent Regt. 1914–1919*, The Medeci Society, 1922

Sellars, Leonard, *The Hood Battalion*, Leo Cooper, 1995

Westlake, Ray, *British Battalions on the Somme*, Leo Cooper, 1995

Westlake, Ray, *British Regiments at Gallipoli*, Leo Cooper, 1996

Williamson, Henry, *How Dear is Life*
A Fox Under My Cloak
The Golden Virgin
Love and the Loveless
A Test to Destruction

Novels that form part of 'A Chronicle of Ancient Sunlight', Macdonald and Co, 1954–60